Remember This?

People, Things and Events
FROM **1943** TO THE **PRESENT DAY**

US EDITION

Rewind, Replay, Remember

What can you remember before you turned six? If you're like most of us, not much: the comforting smell of a blanket or the rough texture of a sweater, perhaps. A mental snapshot of a parent arriving home late at night. A tingle of delight or the shadow of sorrow.

But as we grow out of childhood, our autobiographical and episodic memories—they're the ones hitched to significant events such as birthdays or leaving school—are created and filed more effectively, enabling us to piece them together at a later date. And the more we revisit those memories, the less likely we are to lose the key that unlocks them.

We assemble these fragments into a more-or-less coherent account of our lives—the one we tell to ourselves, our friends, our relatives. And while this one-of-a-kind biopic loses a little definition over the years, some episodes remain in glorious technicolor—although it's usually the most embarrassing incidents!

But this is one movie that's never quite complete. Have you ever had a memory spring back unbidden, triggered by something seemingly unrelated? This book is an attempt to discover those forgotten scenes using the events, sounds, and faces linked to the milestones in your life.

It's time to blow off the cobwebs and see how much you can remember!

It Happened in 1943

The biggest event in the year is one that didn't make the front pages: you were born! Here are some of the national stories that people were talking about.

- Paper Doll tops the radio playlists
- Race riots in Detroit and New York
- The Pentagon dedicated
- Botanist George Washington Carver died
- Electrical engineer Nikola Tesla died
- New York Yankees win the World Series
- FDR first president to travel by airplane on official business
- Golden Globe Awards start
- John F. Kennedy's patrol torpedo boat sunk (right)
- US Mint replaces copper with steel in one-cent coin
- Navy uses ground corn cobs to clean airplane engines
- All-American Girls Professional Baseball League plays
- Dwight D. Eisenhower selected to command Allied armies in Europe
- Slinky invented
- Jefferson Memorial dedicated
- Manhattan Project at Los Alamos begins
- Silly Putty invented
- Stormy Weather premiers
- Casablanca wins Best Picture
- Leonard Bernstein conducts at Carnegie Hall

Born this year:
- Quarterback Joe Namath
- Actor Robert De Niro
- Tennis great Arthur Ashe
- Singer Barry Manilow

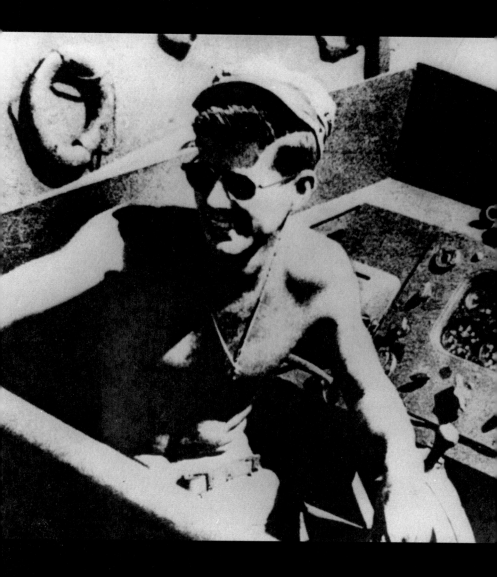

"It was involuntary. They sank my boat." Aged 25, John F. Kennedy's heroism earned him a Purple Heart and a Navy and Marine Corps Medal. It began with the collision between his tiny Patrol Torpedo PT-109 boat (above) and a huge Japanese destroyer, a tragedy in which two men were killed. A six-day ordeal of island hopping, perilous swims and even a message carved on a coconut shell eventually brought JFK and his men back to safety. The wreckage of PT-109 was found in 2002.

On the Bookshelf
When You Were Small

The books of our childhood linger long in the memory. These are the children's classics, all published in your first ten years. Do you remember the stories? What about the covers?

1943	**The Little Prince by Antoine de Saint-Exupéry** In 1935, poet, aristocrat and aviator de Saint-Exupéry crash-landed in the desert. His hallucinations before eventual rescue were the seeds of the story that would later become the bestseller Le Petit Prince.
1944	Prayer for a Child by Rachel Field
1945	Pippi Longstocking by Astrid Lindgren
1945	Stuart Little by E.B. White
1945	The Carrot Seed by Ruth Krauss
1946	**Thomas the Tank Engine by Rev. W. Awdry** Rev. Awdrey appeared in his own books as the Thin Clergyman. His more portly friend in real life, Teddy Boston, appeared by his fictional side—known, of course, as the Fat Clergyman.
1946	Scuffy the Tugboat by Gertrude Crampton
1946	**The Mystery of the Tolling Bell by Carolyn Keene** The Nancy Drew series ran for 175 books. The author of the early titles was adventurer journalist Mildred Wirt Benson. She received a flat fee and no recognition until a 1980 court case unraveled her contribution.
1947	Goodnight Moon by Margaret Wise Brown
1948	Blueberries for Sal by Robert McCloskey
1949	**Bartholomew and the Oobleck by Dr. Seuss** Oobleck is the atrociously gummy substance that rains from the sky in Dr. Seuss's tale, broadly summarized as "be careful what you wish for." Oobleck lives on as the amazing non-Newtonian liquid made from cornstarch.
1949	Song of the Swallows by Leo Politi
1950	Better Known as Johnny Appleseed by Mabel Leigh Hunt
1950	The Lion, the Witch and the Wardrobe by C.S. Lewis
1952	Charlotte's Web by E.B. White

Around the World in Your Birth Year

Here are the events from outside the US that were big enough to make news back home in the year you were born. And you won't remember any of them!

✦ Jewish resistance begins in Warsaw Ghetto
✦ Allies defeat Axis forces in North Africa
✦ Hamburg bombing leaves over 42,000 dead
✦ Fire at Irish orphanage kills 35, mostly children
✦ Allies invade Italy
✦ Popular uprising in Naples drives out Nazi forces
✦ Iraq joins the Allies against Germany
✦ Germany dissolves government and occupies Denmark
✦ Battle of Berlin is fought in the sky
✦ German forces surrender at Stalingrad
✦ RAF uses radar-controlled bombs
✦ Britain uses Colossus computer to break German codes
✦ Assassination attempts on Hitler fail
✦ Mussolini resigns
✦ Paricutin volcano erupts in a corn field
✦ Vicodin is produced
✦ Swiss chemist tries LSD
✦ Churchill addresses US congress
✦ Coup removes Argentina president
✦ Chiang Kai-shek takes oath of Chairman of National China
✦ Charlie Chaplin marries
✦ Italy surrenders to Allied forces
✦ Lebanon gains independence from France
✦ Four allies sign Moscow Declarations
✦ Bengal Famine kills between 1 and 2 million people

Boys' Names When You Were Born

Once upon a time, popular names came... and stuck. (John hogged the top spot for 40 years, to 1924.) These are the most popular names when you were born.

James
James was not only the first choice in 1943, it was the most popular boy's' name of the last hundred years, bestowed upon nearly five million babies (narrowly beating John into second place).

Robert
John
William
Richard
David
Charles
Thomas
Ronald
Michael
Donald
Larry
Joseph
George
Kenneth
Gary
Jerry
Edward
Paul
Dennis
Frank
Raymond
Gerald
Roger

Rising and falling stars:
Gordon was on the way out in 1943, but new Top 100 entrants included Danny, Mike, Steve and Timothy.

Girls' Names When You Were Born

On the girls' side of the maternity ward, Mary and Helen topped the list for decades. But by 1943, Helen had fallen to 28th position and Mary's crown was in the balance…

Mary
Mary was the name chosen for 3 million babies over the last century: twice as many as Patricia, the second most popular pick overall.

Barbara
Patricia
Linda
Carol
Sandra
Judith

Sharon
Eighth place is Sharon's best ever ranking.

Nancy
Betty
Carolyn
Shirley
Judy
Margaret
Karen
Joyce
Donna
Susan
Dorothy
Janet
Joan
Kathleen
Elizabeth
Diane

Rising and falling stars:
Every name in 1943's Top 100 appeared in one or more subsequent years; Dianne, Paula, Pamela and Marcia were fresh faces.

Things People Did When You Were Growing Up...

...that hardly anyone does now. Some of these we remember fondly; others are best left in the past!

- Help Mom make cookies using a cookie press
- Keep bread in a breadbox
- Can and preserve vegetables from your garden
- Listen to daytime soap operas on the radio
- Participate in Church fundraisers
- Watch endurance competitions like flagpole sitting and goldfish eating
- Build scooters from roller skates and scrap wood
- Bring a slide-rule to math class
- Take a Sunday drive out to the country
- Play leapfrog
- Live in a Sears Modern Home ordered from the Sears catalog
- Get a treat from the pharmacy soda fountain
- Camp in a "Hooverville" while looking for work
- Keep a thrift or kitchen garden
- Buy penny candy
- Buy goods from door-to-door salesmen
- Wear clothing made from flour sacks
- Collect marbles
- Join a dance marathon
- Listen to Amos n' Andy on the radio on weekend evenings
- Eat Water Pie
- "Window shop" downtown on Saturdays
- Pitch pennies
- Earn $30 a month plus food and shelter working for the Civilian Conservation Corps

How Many of These Games Are Still Played?

The first half of the 20th century was the heyday for new board and card games launched to the US public. Some are still firm family favorites, but which ones did you play when you were young?

1925	Pegity
1925	Playing for the Cup
1927	Hokum ("The game for a roomful")
1920s	The Greyhound Racing Game
1930	Wahoo
1932	Finance
1934	Sorry!
1935	**Monopoly**

Monopoly
The game's origins lie with The Landlord's Game, patented in 1904 by Elizabeth Magie. (The anti-monopoly version—Prosperity—didn't catch on.) It was the first game with a never-ending path rather than a fixed start and finish.

1935	Easy Money
1936	The Amazing Adventures of Fibber McGee
1937	Meet the Missus
1937	Stock Ticker
1938	Scrabble
1938	Movie Millions
1940	Dig
1940	Prowl Car
1942	Sea Raider
1943	Chutes and Ladders
1949	**Clue**

Clue
Clue—or Cluedo, as it is known to most outside the USA—introduced us to a host of shady characters and grisly murder weapons. For years those included a piece of genuine lead pipe, now replaced on health grounds.

1949	**Candy Land**

Candy Land
This wholesome family racing game, invented on a polio ward, was the victim of something less savory nearly 50 years after its launch when an adult website claimed the domain name. Thankfully, the courts swiftly intervened.

Things People Do Now...

...that were virtually unknown when you were young.
How many of these habits are part of your routine or even
second nature these days? Do you remember the first time?

- Get curbside grocery pickup
- Stream movies instead of going to Blockbuster for a rental
- Learn remotely and online
- Communicate by text or video chat
- Use a Kindle or other e-reading device
- Go geocaching
- Track your sleep, exercise, or fertility with a watch
- Use a weighted blanket
- Use a robotic/automatic vacuum
- Take your dog to a dog park
- Have a package delivered by drone
- Find a date online or through an app
- Use hand sanitizer
- Automatically soothe your baby with a self-rocking bassinet
- Host a gender-reveal party during pregnancy
- Use a home essential oil diffuser or salt lamp
- Have a "destination wedding"
- Use a device charging station while waiting for a flight
- Get a ride from Uber or Lyft instead of a taxi
- Drink hard seltzer
- Take a home DNA test (for you... or your pet)
- Have a telemedicine/virtual healthcare visit
- Smoke an e-cigarette/"vape"
- Start your car, dryer, or air conditioner via an app

Popular Food in the 1950s

For many, the post-war years meant more of one thing in particular on the table: meat. In the yard, men stepped up to the barbeque to sharpen their skills. In the kitchen, fancy new electric appliances and frozen TV dinners promised convenience and new, exotic flavors.

Tuna noodle casserole

Dinty Moore Beef Stew

Beef stroganoff

Green bean casserole

Green bean casserole was invented in the Campbell's test kitchen in 1955 as a cheap, fuss-free dish. Today, around 40 percent of Campbell's Cream of Mushroom soup sold in the US goes into this dinner table staple.

Pigs-in-a-blanket

Pigs get different blankets in the United Kingdom, where sausages are wrapped in bacon rather than pastry.

Backyard barbecues

Ovaltine

Swedish meatballs

Pineapple upside down cake

Spam

Ground pork shoulder and ham sold in a distinctive can—for much of the world, that means Spam. This "meatloaf without basic training" is affordable and still popular, with over eight billion cans sold since it was first sold in 1937.

Ambrosia salad

Sugar Smacks

Cheez Whiz

Stuffed celery

Campbell's Tomato Soup spice cake

Swanson Turkey TV Dinners

Dreamed up as a solution to an over-supply of turkey, TV dinners proved nearly as popular as the TV itself. Swanson sold over 25 million of them in 1954, the year these handy meal packs were launched.

Veg-All canned vegetables

Chicken à la King

Cars of the 1950s

Was this the golden age of automobiles? In truth, some of these models had been brought to market long before, such as the Buick Roadmaster and the Studebaker Champion. But even stalwarts were quick to adopt the Space Age theme of the decade as sweeping lines, tailfins, and cascading chrome grilles became the norm.

1926	Chrysler Imperial
1936	General Motors Buick Roadmaster
1939	**Studebaker Champion** Over seven decades, the Champion's creator, Raymond Loewy, designed railroads, logos, buses, vending machines, and a space station for NASA.
1939	Chrysler DeSoto Custom
1947	Studebaker Starlight Coupe
1948	**Crosley Station Wagon** The first car to be marketed as "Sports Utility."
1948	Jaguar XK120
1949	**Muntz Jet** Fewer than 200 Muntz Jets were built by founder Madman Muntz, an engineer who married seven times and made (and lost) fortunes selling cars, TVs, and more.
1949	Chrysler Dodge Coronet
1950	General Motors Chevrolet Bel-Air
1950	Nash Rambler
1951	Hudson Hornet
1953	General Motors Chevrolet Corvette
1953	General Motors Buick Skylark
1953	General Motors Cadillac Eldorado
1953	Nash Metropolitan
1954	Ford Skyliner
1955	Ford Thunderbird
1955	Ford Fairlane
1956	Studebaker Golden Hawk
1956	Chrysler Plymouth Fury
1957	**Mercedes-Benz 300 SL Roadster** Voted "Sports Car of the Century" in 1999.

Cars crawl out of 1950s Philadelphia over the Ben Franklin Bridge. Henry Ford wasn't the only one to "build a car for the great multitude." Millions of new suburbanites embraced their newfound freedom—even if that meant driving to the same place as everyone else.

The Biggest Hits When You Were 10

Whistled by your father, hummed by your sister or overheard on the radio, these are the hit records as you reached double digits.

Tony Bennett ♪ Rags to Riches
Hank Williams ♪ Your Cheatin' Heart
Les Paul and Mary Ford ♪ Vaya con Dios
Teresa Brewer ♪ Till I Waltz Again with You
Dean Martin ♪ That's Amore
Patti Page ♪ (How Much Is)
That Doggie in the Window?
Joni James ♪ Have You Heard?
Eartha Kitt ♪ C'est Si Bon
Nat King Cole ♪ Pretend
Big Mama Thornton ♪ Hound Dog
Frank Sinatra ♪ I've Got the World on a String
Jim Reeves ♪ Mexican Joe
The Davis Sisters ♪ I Forgot More Than You'll Ever Know
Eddie Fisher ♪ With These Hands
Ray Anthony and His Orchestra ♪ Dragnet
Carl Smith ♪ Hey Joe
Ray Charles ♪ Mess Around
Percy Faith and His Orchestra ♪ The Song from Moulin Rouge
Fats Domino ♪ Please Don't Leave Me
Perry Como ♪ Don't Let the Stars Get in Your Eyes
Eddie Fisher ♪ I'm Walking Behind You
The Hilltoppers ♪ P.S. I Love You
Frankie Laine ♪ I Believe
Bill Haley and His Comets ♪ Crazy Man, Crazy

Faster, Easier, Better

Yesterday's technological breakthrough is today's modern convenience. Here are some of the lab and engineering marvels that were made before you turned 21 years old.

1943	Kidney dialysis machine
1944	Programmable calculator
1945	Cruise control in cars
1946	**Waterproof diaper**

The inventor of the first waterproof diaper, the Boater, was told repeatedly that no one wanted it and no one had been asking for such a thing. She decided to manufacture it herself and the product was an immediate success.

1947	Transistor
1948	Computer program
1949	Wurlitzer Select-O-Matic jukebox
1949	Zamboni ice resurfacer
1950	Teleprompter
1951	Wetsuit
1952	Artificial heart
1953	Heart-lung machine
1954	Acoustic suspension loudspeaker
1955	Pocket transistor radio
1956	Hard Disk Drive
1956	Operating system (OS)
1957	Laser
1958	Microchip
1959	Weather satellite
1960	Global navigation satellite system
1961	Spreadsheet (electronic)
1962	Red LED
1963	**Computer mouse**

The inventor of the computer mouse had patented it in 1963. However, by the time the mouse became commercially available in the 1980s, his patent had expired. The first computer system with a mouse came from Xerox in 1981. It offered a mouse much larger than the model seen now.

Across the Nation

Double digits at last: you're old enough to eavesdrop on adults and scan the headlines. These may be some of the earliest national news stories you remember.

- Dr. Jonas Salk announces polio vaccine
- Ethel and Julius Rosenberg executed for espionage
- Department of Health, Education, and Welfare created
- President ends all wage and price control
- Pilot Chuck Yeager sets new speed record
- Evidence found linking smoking with cancer
- New York Yankees win 5th consecutive World Series
- Supreme Court rules baseball is a sport, not a business
- Color TVs hit the market
- Transistor radios go on sale
- Town renames itself Jim Thorpe
- Korean War ends
- Eisenhower inaugurated
- Earl Warren appointed to Supreme Court
- Atomic Bomb tourism begins
- Frozen French fries become available
- TV dinners offered
- Hank Williams died
- Cinemascope used in movies
- Lucille Ball gives birth to son
- Matchbox cars introduced
- Speedbump designed
- Call sign "Air Force One" created
- Peeps candy goes on sale

Born this year:
- Actress Kim Basinger
- Wrestler Hulk Hogan
- Singer Cyndi Lauper

Kapow! Comic Books and Heroes from Your Childhood

Barely a year went past in the mid-20th Century without a new super-powered hero arriving to save the day. Here are some that were taking on the bad guys during your childhood.

Mickey Mouse ✴ Mickey Mouse
The Flash ✴ Jay Garrick
Adventure Comics ✴ Aquaman
Venus ✴ Venus
Casper The Friendly Ghost ✴ Casper
Strange Adventures ✴ Captain Comet
Donald Duck ✴ Donald Duck
Uncle Scrooge ✴ Uncle Scrooge
Phantom Stranger ✴ Phantom Stranger
Wonder Woman ✴ Wonder Woman
Action Comics ✴ Superman
Detective Comics ✴ Batman
Rawhide Kid ✴ Rawhide Kid
Showcase ✴ Barry Allen
World's Finest Comics ✴ Superman
Patsy Walker ✴ Patsy Walker
Kid Colt, Outlaw ✴ Kid Colt

Winners of the Stanley Cup Since You Were Born

The prestigious Stanley Cup has been changing hands since 1893, although the trophy itself has been redesigned more than once. Here are the teams to lift the champagne-filled cup since you were born.

- **Detroit Red Wings (9)**
  1955: 18-year-old Larry Hillman became the youngest player to have his name engraved on the Stanley Cup trophy.

- Chicago Black Hawks (4)

- **Boston Bruins (3)**
  1970: Bobby Orr scored perhaps the most famous goal in NHL history, in midair, to clinch the title.

- **New York Rangers (1)**
  After a 1940 victory, the Rangers would not win another Stanley Cup for another 54 years.

- Toronto Maple Leafs (9)
- Montreal Canadiens (20)
- Philadelphia Flyers (2)
- New York Islanders (4)
- Edmonton Oilers (5)
- **Calgary Flames (1)**
  1989 was the last time a Stanley Cup Final has been played between two teams from Canada.

- Pittsburgh Penguins (5)
- New Jersey Devils (3)
- **Colorado Avalanche (3)**
  1996: A win in their first season after moving from Quebec (where their nickname was the Nordiques).

- Dallas Stars (1)
- Tampa Bay Lightning (3)
- Carolina Hurricanes (1)
- Anaheim Ducks (1)
- Los Angeles Kings (2)
- Washington Capitals (1)
- St. Louis Blues (1)

On the Silver Screen When You Were 11

From family favorites to the films you weren't allowed to watch, these are the films and actors that drew the praise and the crowds when you turned 11.

White Christmas  Bing Crosby, Danny Kaye, Rosemary Clooney
Dial M for Murder  Ray Milland, Grace Kelly, Robert Cummings
Diary of a
Country Priest  Claude Laydu, Jean Riveyre, Adrien Borel
Ugetsu Monogatari  Masayuki Mori, Machiko Kyo, Kinuyo Tanaka
Demetrius
and the Gladiators  Victor Mature, Susan Hayward, Michael Rennie
The Caine Mutiny  Humphrey Bogart, Jose Ferrer, Van Johnson
The month it premiered, Humphrey Bogart appeared on the cover of Time Magazine.

The High
and the Mighty  John Wayne, Claire Trevor, Laraine Day
20,000 Leagues
Under the Sea  Kirk Douglas, James Mason, Paul Lukas
Seven Brides for
Seven Brothers  Howard Keel, Jane Powell, Jeff Richards
Vera Cruz  Gary Cooper, Burt Lancaster, Ernest Borgnine
Mari Blanchard was set to play the female lead, but there was a clause forbidding her from appearing on television.

There's No Business
Like Show Business  Ethel Merman, Dan Dailey, Donald O'Connor
Creature from
The Black Lagoon  Richard Carlson, Julie Adams, Richard Denning
On the Waterfront  Marlon Brando, Karl Malden, Lee J. Cobb
Rear Window  James Stewart, Grace Kelly, Wendell Corey
A Star is Born  Judy Garland, James Mason, Jack Carlson
Them!  James Whitmore, Edmund Gwenn, Joan Weldon
Three Coins
in the Fountain  Clifton Webb, Dorothy McGuire, Jean Peters
The Barefoot Contessa  Humphrey Bogart, Ava Gardner, Edmond O'Brien
Carmen Jones  Harry Belafonte, Dorothy Dandridge, Pearl Bailey

Comic Strips You'll Know

Comic strips took off in the late 19th century and for much of the 20th century they were a dependable feature of everyday life. Some were solo efforts; others became so-called zombie strips, living on well beyond their creator. A century on, some are still going. But how many from your youth will you remember?

1940–52	The Spirit by Will Eisner
1930–	**Blondie** In 1995, Blondie was one of 20 strips commemorated by the US Postal Service in the Comic Strip Classics series.
1931–	**Dick Tracy** Gould's first idea? A detective called Plainclothes Tracy.
1930–95	Mickey Mouse
1932–	Mary Worth
1936–	**The Phantom** Lee Falk worked on The Phantom for 63 years and Mandrake The Magician for 65.
1919–	Barney Google and Snuffy Smith
1938–	Nancy
1946–	Mark Trail
1937–	**Prince Valiant** Edward, the Duke of Windsor (previously Edward VIII), called Prince Valiant the "greatest contribution to English literature in the past hundred years."
1934–2003	**Flash Gordon** Alex Raymond created Flash Gordon to compete with the Buck Rogers comic strip.
1934–77	Li'l Abner by Al Capp
1925–74	Etta Kett by Paul Robinson
1947–69	Grandma by Charles Kuhn
1948–	Rex Morgan, M.D.
1933–87	Brick Bradford
1950–2000	**Peanuts by Charles M. Schulz** Schultz was inducted into the Hockey Hall of Fame after building the Redwood Empire Arena near his studio.
1950–	Beetle Bailey

Biggest Hits by The King

He may have conquered rock'n'roll, but Elvis's success straddled genres including country music, R&B, and more. These are his Number 1s from across the charts, beginning with the rockabilly "I Forgot…" through the posthumous country hit, "Guitar Man."

I Forgot to Remember to Forget (1955)
Heartbreak Hotel (1956)
I Want You, I Need You, I Love You (1956)
Don't Be Cruel (1956)
Hound Dog (1956)
Love Me Tender (1956)
Too Much (1957)
All Shook Up (1957)
(Let Me Be Your) Teddy Bear (1957)
Jailhouse Rock (1957)
Don't (1957)
Wear My Ring Around Your Neck (1958)
Hard Headed Woman (1958)
A Big Hunk O' Love (1959)
Stuck On You (1960)
It's Now or Never (1960)
Are You Lonesome Tonight? (1960)
Surrender (1961)
Good Luck Charm (1962)
Suspicious Minds (1969)
Moody Blue (1976)
Way Down (1977)
Guitar Man (1981)

Childhood Candies

In labs across the country, mid-century food scientists dreamed up new and colorful ways to delight children just like you. These are the fruits of their labor, launched before you turned twenty-one.

1945	Dots (Mason Company)
1946	Almond Joy (Peter Paul)
1947	Bazooka Bubble Gum (Topps Candy Company)
1949	Jolly Rancher (Jolly Rancher Company)
1949	Junior Mints (James O. Welch Company)
1949	**Whoppers** (Overland Candy Company) **Whoppers were known as "Giants" before 1949.**
1949	Smarties (Ce De Candy, Inc.)
1950	Cup-O-Gold (Hoffman Candy Company)
1950	Red Vines (American Licorice Co.)
1950	Hot Tamales (Just Born)
1950	Rocky Road Candy Bar (The Annabell Candy Co.)
1952	Pixy Stix (Sunline, Inc.)
1954	Atomic Fireballs (Ferrera Candy Co.)
1954	**Marshmallow Peeps** (Just Born) **Today it takes six minutes to make one Peep, but when the candy was first introduced, it took 27 hours!**
1954	Peanut M&Ms (Mars)
1955	**Chick-O-Sticks** (Atkinson's) **These candies were called "Chicken Bones" until they were renamed in 1955.**
1950s	Swedish Fish (Malaco)
1950s	Look! Candy Bar (Golden Nugget Candy Co.)
1960	Sixlets (Leaf Brands)
1962	Now and Later (Phoenix Candy Company)
1962	**SweeTarts** (Sunline, Inc.) **These have the same candy base as Pixy Stix which was invented using drink powder from a children's drink.**
1962	LemonHead (Ferrara Candy Company)
1963	**Cadbury Creme Eggs** (Fry's) **An original 1963 Fry's Creme Egg (as they were then called) was discovered in 2017. It hasn't been eaten.**

Books of the Decade

Ten years of your life that took you from adventure books aged 10 to dense works of profundity at 20—or perhaps just grown-up adventures! How many did you read when they were first published?

1953	Fahrenheit 451 by Ray Bradbury
1953	The Adventures of Augie March by Saul Bellow
1954	The Fellowship of the Ring by J.R.R. Tolkien
1954	Under the Net by Iris Murdoch
1955	Lolita by Vladimir Nabokov
1955	The Ginger Man by J.P. Donleavy
1955	The Two Towers by J.R.R. Tolkien
1956	Peyton Place by Grace Metalious
1956	Giovanni's Room by James Baldwin
1956	The Return of the King by J.R.R. Tolkien
1957	On the Road by Jack Kerouac
1957	Atlas Shrugged by Ayn Rand
1958	Breakfast at Tiffany's by Truman Capote
1958	Doctor Zhivago by Boris Pasternak
1958	Exodus by Leon Uris
1959	The Haunting of Hill House by Shirley Jackson
1959	Naked Lunch by William S. Burroughs
1959	Advise and Consent by Allen Drury
1960	To Kill a Mockingbird by Harper Lee
1960	Hawaii by James Michener
1961	Catch-22 by Joseph Heller
1961	Stranger in a Strange Land by Robert A. Heinlein
1962	One Flew Over the Cuckoo's Nest by Ken Kesey
1962	Franny and Zooey by J.D. Salinger

US Buildings

Some were loathed then, loved now; others, the reverse. Some broke new architectural ground; others housed famous or infamous businesses, or helped to power a nation. All of them were built in your first 18 years.

1943	The Pentagon
1944	Geneva Steel Mill, Utah
1945	Pacific Gas and Electric Company General Office Building and Annex, SF
1946	**Flamingo Hotel, Las Vegas** The Presidential Suite at The Flamingo originally featured a few extras by request of its mobster owner, "Bugsy" Siegel: bulletproof glass and a secret escape ladder. Siegel was shot dead in Beverly Hills.
1947	75 Rockefeller Plaza
1948	Mile High Stadium, Denver
1949	Promontory Apartments, Chicago
1950	Metropolitan Life North Building
1951	US General Accounting Office Building
1952	United Nations Secretariat Building
1953	Sullivan Tower, Nashville
1954	Republic Center, Dallas
1955	One Prudential Plaza, Chicago
1956	**Capitol Records Building, Los Angeles** The world's first circular office building.
1957	666 Fifth Avenue, New York City
1958	Time & Life Building, New York City
1959	2 Broadway, New York City
1960	Four Gateway Center, Pittsburgh
1961	One Chase Manhattan Plaza

Radio DJs from Your Childhood

If the radio was the soundtrack to your life as you grew up, some of these voices were part of the family. (The stations listed are where these DJs made their name; the dates are their radio broadcasting career).

Wolfman Jack 🎙 XERB/Armed Forces Radio (1960–1995)

Jocko Henderson 🎙 WDAS/W LIB (1952–1991)

Casey Kasem 🎙 KRLA (1954–2010)
Kasem was the host of American Top 40 for four decades.
By 1986, his show was broadcast on 1,000 radio stations.

Bruce Morrow 🎙 WABC (1959-)

Murray Kaufman 🎙 WINS (1958–1975)
You'll likely remember him as Murray the K, the self-declared
"fifth Beatle" (he played a lot of music from the Fab Four).

Alison Steele 🎙 WNEW-FM (1966–1995)
Aka The Nightbird, Steele was that rarity of the sixties
and seventies: a successful female DJ.

Alan Freed 🎙 WJW/WINS (1945–1965)
Freed's career crashed after he was found to have been
taking payola. His contribution was recognized posthumously
when admitted into the Rock n Roll Hall of Fame.

Robert W. Morgan 🎙 KHJ-AM (1955–1998)

Dan Ingram 🎙 WABC (1958–2004)

Dave Hull 🎙 KRLA (1955–2010)
Another candidate for the "fifth Beatle," Hull interviewed
the band many times.

Hal Jackson 🎙 WBLS (1940–2011)

Johnny Holliday 🎙 KYA (1956-)

Herb Kent 🎙 WVON (1944–2016)
"Cool Gent" Herb Kent was the
longest-serving DJ on the radio.

Tom Donahue 🎙 WIBG/KYA (1949–1975)

John R. 🎙 WLAC (1941–1973)

Bill Randle 🎙 WERE/WCBS (1940s–2004)

Jack Spector 🎙 WMCA (1955–1994)
Spector, one of WMCA's "Good Guys," died on air in 1994.
A long silence after playing "I'm in the Mood for Love"
alerted station staff.

It Happened in 1959

Here's a round-up of the most newsworthy events from across the US in the year you turned (sweet) 16.

- ✦ Alaska declared the 49th state
- ✦ Titan missile launched at Cape Canaveral
- ✦ Weather satellite launched
- ✦ NASA announces the Mercury Seven (right)
- ✦ Saint Lawrence Seaway opens for shipping
- ✦ Hawaii admitted as 50th state
- ✦ Heart defibrillator developed
- ✦ Antarctic Treaty signed
- ✦ Coppertone girl appears in ads
- ✦ Barbie doll released
- ✦ Microchip invented
- ✦ The Day the Music Died
- ✦ Motown records founded
- ✦ Monkey astronauts recovered safely
- ✦ Richard Nixon debates Nikita Khrushchev in the "kitchen"
- ✦ Clutter family murdered "in cold blood"
- ✦ George Reeves—the original Superman—dies mysteriously
- ✦ Pioneer 4 leaves Earth's orbit
- ✦ Guggenheim Museum completed
- ✦ Picture of Earth taken from orbit
- ✦ Labor Management Reporting and Disclosure Act passed
- ✦ Grammy awards begin
- ✦ Jack Nicklaus wins USGA golf championship
- ✦ Commercial copier launched

Born this year:
- ⮑ Vice President Mike Pence
- ⮑ Basketball star Magic Johnson
- ⮑ Designer Michael Kors

NASA

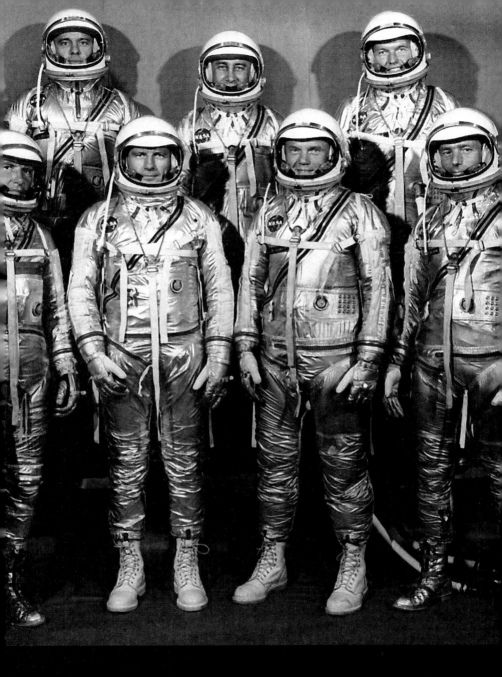

Drawn from the ranks of military test pilots, these were the men chosen to discover if humans could survive weightless flight: the Mercury Seven.
Front row, l-r: Walter M. Schirra Jr., Donald K. "Deke" Slayton, John H. Glenn Jr., and M. Scott Carpenter.
Back row: Alan B. Shepard Jr., Virgil I. "Gus" Grissom, and L. Gordon Cooper Jr.

News Anchors of the Fifties and Sixties

Trusted, familiar, and exclusively male: these are the faces that brought you the news, and the catchphrases they made their own.

Edward R. Murrow 📺 CBS (1938-59)
"Good night, and good luck."

Walter Cronkite 📺 CBS (1962-81)
"And that's the way it is."

David Brinkley 📺 NBC (1956-71)
"Good night, Chet..."

Chet Huntley 📺 NBC (1956-70)
"...Good night, David."

Harry Reasoner 📺 CBS & ABC (1961-91)
Frank Reynolds 📺 ABC (1968-70)

John Charles Daly 📺 CBS & ABC (1941-60)
"Good night and a good tomorrow."

Douglas Edwards 📺 CBS (1948-62)
Hugh Downs 📺 NBC (1962-71)
John Chancellor 📺 NBC (1970-82)

Paul Harvey 📺 ABC Radio (1951-2009)
"Hello Americans, this is Paul Harvey. Stand by for news!"

Mike Wallace 📺 CBS (1963-66)

John Cameron Swayze 📺 NBC (1948-56)
"Well, that's the story, folks! This is John Cameron Swayze, and I'm glad we could get together."

Ron Cochran 📺 ABC (1962-65)
Bob Young 📺 ABC (1967-68)
Dave Garroway 📺 NBC (1952-61)
Bill Shadel 📺 ABC (1960-63)

Fifties Game Shows

It all started so well: appointment radio became appointment TV, with new and crossover game shows bringing us together. But as the decade progressed, the scandal emerged: some shows were fixed. Quiz shows were down, but certainly not out. (Dates include periods off-air.)

Break the Bank 🎙 (1945–57)

Beat The Clock 🎙 (1950–2019)

Name That Tune 🎙 (1952–85)
A radio crossover that spawned 25 international versions.

Strike It Rich 🎙 (1947–58)

The Price Is Right 🎙 (1956–65)
The original version of the current quiz that began in 1972. This one was hosted by Bill Cullen.

Down You Go 🎙 (1951–56)

I've Got A Secret 🎙 (1952–2006)

What's The Story 🎙 (1951–55)

The $64,000 Question 🎙 (1955–58)

People Are Funny 🎙 (1942–60)

Tic-Tac-Dough 🎙 (1956–90)
Early Tic-Tac-Dough contestants were often coached; around three-quarters of the shows in one run were rigged.

The Name's The Same 🎙 (1951–55)

Two For The Money 🎙 (1952–57)

The Big Payoff 🎙 (1951–62)

Twenty-One 🎙 (1956–58)
At the heart of the rigging scandal, Twenty-One was the subject of Robert Redford's 1994 movie, Quiz Show.

Masquerade Party 🎙 (1952–60)

You Bet Your Life 🎙 (1947–61)
A comedy quiz hosted by Groucho Marx.

Truth or Consequences 🎙 (1940–88)
Started life as a radio quiz. TV host Bob Barker signed off with: "Hoping all your consequences are happy ones."

20 Questions 🎙 (1946–55)

What's My Line 🎙 (1950–75)

Liberty Issue Stamps

First released in 1954, the Liberty Issue drew its name from not one but three depictions of the Statue of Liberty across the denominations. (There was only room for one "real" woman, though.) It coincided with the new era of stamp collecting as a childhood hobby that endured for decades. Were you one of these new miniature philatelists?

Benjamin Franklin ½ ¢ 🖾 Polymath (writer, inventor, scientist)
**Franklin discovered the principle of electricity,
the Law of Conservation of Charge.**

George Washington 1 ¢ 🖾 First US President
Palace of the Governors 1 ¼ ¢ 🖾
**A building in Santa Fe, New Mexico that served as
the seat of government of New Mexico for centuries.**

Mount Vernon 1 ½ ¢ 🖾 George Washington's plantation
Thomas Jefferson 2 ¢ 🖾 Polymath; third US President
Bunker Hill Monument 2 ½ ¢ 🖾 Battle site of the Revolutionary War
Statue of Liberty 3 ¢ 🖾 Gifted by the people of France
Abraham Lincoln 4 ¢ 🖾 16th US President
**Lincoln received a patent for a flotation device that assisted
boats in moving through shallow water.**

The Hermitage 4 ½ ¢ 🖾 Andrew Jackson's plantation
James Monroe 5 ¢ 🖾 Fifth US President
Theodore Roosevelt 6 ¢ 🖾 26th US President
Woodrow Wilson 7 ¢ 🖾 28th US President; served during WW1
John J. Pershing 8 ¢ 🖾 US Army officer during World War I
Alamo 9 ¢ 🖾 Site of a pivotal Texas Revolution battle
Independence Hall 10 ¢ 🖾 Independence declared here
Benjamin Harrison 12 ¢ 🖾 23rd US President
John Jay 15 ¢ 🖾 First Chief Justice of the United States
Monticello 20 ¢ 🖾 Thomas Jefferson's plantation
Paul Revere 25 ¢ 🖾 Alerted militia of the British approach
Robert E. Lee 30 ¢ 🖾 Confederate general in the Civil War
John Marshall 40 ¢ 🖾 Fourth Chief Justice of the US
Susan B. Anthony 50 ¢ 🖾 Women's suffrage activist
Patrick Henry $1 🖾 Leader of the Dec. of Independence
Alexander Hamilton $5 🖾 First Secretary of the Treasury

The Biggest Hits When You Were 16

The artists that topped the charts when you turned 16 might not be in your top 10 these days, but you'll probably remember them!

The Platters 🎵 Smoke Gets in Your Eyes
The Isley Brothers 🎵 Shout!
Johnny Horton 🎵 The Battle of New Orleans
Bobby Darin 🎵 Mack the Knife
Ray Charles and His Orchestra 🎵 What'd I Say
Lloyd Price 🎵 Stagger Lee
James Brown
and the Famous Flames 🎵 Try Me
The Coasters 🎵 Charlie Brown
Marty Robbins 🎵 El Paso
Henry Mancini
and His Orchestra 🎵 Peter Gunn Theme
Bobby Darin 🎵 Dream Lover
Dion and the Belmonts 🎵 A Teenager in Love
Jim Reeves 🎵 Billy Bayou
Johnny Cash 🎵 Don't Take Your Guns to Town
Marilyn Monroe 🎵 I Wanna Be Loved by You
The Drifters 🎵 There Goes My Baby
Ricky Nelson 🎵 Never Be Anyone Else but You
The Flamingos 🎵 I Only Have Eyes for You
Frankie Avalon 🎵 Venus
Connie Francis 🎵 My Happiness
Phil Phillips
with the Twilights 🎵 Sea of Love
Paul Anka 🎵 Put Your Head on My Shoulder
Ritchie Valens 🎵 Donna
George Jones 🎵 White Lightning

Medical Advances Before You Were 21

A baby born in 1920 USA had a life expectancy of just 55.4 years. By 2000 that was up to 76.8, thanks to medical advances including many of these.

1943	Kidney dialysis
1944	Disposable catheter
1944	Asperger syndrome (described)
1945	Oral penicillin
1946	All-glass syringe (easier sterilization)
1947	Defibrillation
1949	Intraocular lens (myopia and cataracts)
1950	**Polio vaccine** Jonas Salk was asked about taking a patent on the polio vaccine. He replied, "Can you patent the sun?"
1951	Munchhausen syndrome (described)
1952	Cloning
1953	Ultrasound
1954	Kidney transplant
1955	Mass immunization of polio
1956	**Metered-dose inhaler** Invented after the teen daughter of head of Riker Labs asked why her asthma medicine couldn't be in a can like hair spray. At the time, asthma medicine was given in ineffective squeeze bulb glass containers.
1958	Pacemaker
1959	Bone marrow transplant
1959	In vitro fertilization
1960	CPR
1960	The pill
1960	Coronary artery bypass surgery
1962	Hip replacement
1962	Beta blocker
1962	First oral polio vaccine (Sabin)
1963	Liver transplant

Blockbuster Movies When You Were 16

These are the movies that everyone was talking about. How many of them did you see (or have you seen since)?

North by Northwest 🎬 Cary Grant, Eva Marie Saint, James Mason
Reportedly inspired the name for the annual live music festival, South by Southwest.

Solomon and Sheba 🎬 Yul Brynner, Gina Lollobrigida, George Sanders

Sleeping Beauty 🎬 Mary Costa, Bill Shirley, Eleanor Audley

The Shaggy Dog 🎬 Fred MacMurray, Jean Hagen, Tommy Kirk

Rio Bravo 🎬 John Wayne, Dean Martin, Ricky Nelson

Some Like it Hot 🎬 Marilyn Monroe, Tony Curtis, Jack Lemmon

Imitation of Life 🎬 Lana Turner, Juanita Moore, John Gavin

The Nun's Story 🎬 Audrey Hepburn, Peter Finch, Edith Evans

A Hole in the Head 🎬 Frank Sinatra, Edward G. Robinson, Eleanor Parker

Pillow Talk 🎬 Rock Hudson, Doris Day, Tony Randall
Hudson recorded a message that would play for callers who responded to newspaper and magazine ads for the film.

On the Beach 🎬 Gregory Peck, Ava Gardner, Fred Astaire

Ben-Hur 🎬 Charlton Heston, Jack Hawkins, Haya Harareet

Journey to the Center of the Earth 🎬 James Mason, Pat Boone, Arlene Dahl

Operation Petticoat 🎬 Cary Grant, Tony Curtis, Joan O'Brien

Anatomy of a Murder 🎬 James Stewart, Lee Remick, Ben Gazzara

The Best of Everything 🎬 Hope Lange, Diane Baker, Suzy Parker

Compulsion 🎬 Orson Welles, Diane Varsi, Dean Stockwell

The Diary of Anne Frank 🎬 Millie Perkins, Joseph Schildkraut

Ride Lonesome 🎬 Randolph Scott, Karen Steele, Pernell Roberts

Pork Chop Hill 🎬 Gregory Peck, Rip Torn, George Shibata

The Giant Behemoth 🎬 Gene Evans, Andre Morell, John Turner

Suddenly, Last Summer 🎬 Katharine Hepburn, Elizabeth Taylor, Montgomery Clift

The Young Philadelphians 🎬 Paul Newman, Barbara Rush, Alexis Smith

Game Show Hosts of the Fifties and Sixties

Many of these men were semi-permanent fixtures, their voices and catchphrases ringing through the decades. Some were full-time entertainers; others were on sabbatical from more serious news duties.

John Charles Daly ⋈ What's My Line (1950–67)

Art Linkletter ⋈ People Are Funny (1943–60)

Garry Moore ⋈ I've Got A Secret (1956–64)

Groucho Marx ⋈ You Bet Your Life (1949–61)

Warren Hull ⋈ Strike It Rich (1947–58)

Herb Shriner ⋈ Two For The Money (1952–56)

George DeWitt ⋈ Name That Tune (1953–59)

Robert Q. Lewis ⋈ Name's The Same (1951–54)

Bill Cullen ⋈ The Price Is Right (1956–65)

Walter Cronkite ⋈ It's News To Me (1954)
"The most trusted man in America" was briefly the host of this topical quiz game. He didn't do it again.

Bill Slater ⋈ 20 Questions (1949–52)

Walter Kiernan ⋈ Who Said That (1951–54)

Bob Eubanks ⋈ The Newlywed Game (1966–74)

Bud Collyer ⋈ To Tell The Truth (1956–69)

Jack Barry ⋈ Twenty-One (1956–58)

Bert Parks ⋈ Break The Bank (1945–57)

Hugh Downs ⋈ Concentration (1958–69)

Mike Stokey ⋈ Pantomime Quiz (1947–59)

Allen Ludden ⋈ Password (1961–75)

Bob Barker ⋈ Truth or Consequences (1956–74)
Barker also spent 35 years hosting The Price Is Right.

Hal March ⋈ $64,000 Question (1955–58)

Monty Hall ⋈ Let's Make A Deal (1963–91)
Monty—born "Monte", but misspelled on an early publicity photo—was also a philanthropist who raised around $1 billion over his lifetime.

Johnny Carson ⋈ Who Do You Trust? (1957–63)

Kitchen Inventions

The 20th-century kitchen was a playground for food scientists and engineers with new labor-saving devices and culinary shortcuts launched every year. These all made their debut before you were 18.

1943	Uncle Ben's rice
1944	Dish drying cabinet
1945	Minute Maid orange concentrate
1946	Food processor
1946	Tupperware products
1947	Zen Rex speed peeler
1948	Aluminum foil
1949	**Reddi-Wip cream**

Reddi-Wip has been chosen as one of The Top 100 consumer inventions of 20th century and made its inventor, Aaron Lapin, the 'Whipped Cream King', millions of dollars.

1950	Green Garbage Bags
1951	Kenwood food mixer
1952	Automatic coffee pot
1952	Bread clip
1953	Combination washer-dryer
1954	Zipper storage bag
1955	Lint roller
1956	Saran wrap
1957	Homemaker tableware
1958	Rice-a-Roni
1959	Chocolate Velvet Cake invented
1960	**Automated dishwasher**

Electric dishwashers debuted in 1929 but to little acclaim, due in part to the Great Depression and WWII. Automated models with a drying element finally became popular in the 1970s.

Around the World When You Turned 18

These are the headlines from around the globe as you were catapulted into adulthood.

- East Germans close the border and build the Wall
- Sweden salvages the Vasa warship that sank in the 1600s
- Soviets test largest man-made explosion ever made
- German solves genetic code
- Nureyev defects
- Eichmann goes on trial
- World Wildlife Fund is formed
- Gagarin orbits the Earth
- Probe launches headed to Venus
- Brazil creates national park
- UN condemns South African Apartheid
- Amnesty International is founded
- Portuguese rebels hijack passenger liner
- Volcanic eruption forces evacuation of Tristan da Cunha
- South Africa becomes republic
- UK convicts members of Soviet spy ring
- Monza Italian Grand Prix Race crash kills 14 people
- Coup in Turkey overthrows the government
- Rebels in El Salvador temporarily rule
- China buys $60 million of Canadian grain
- Tram service ceases in Sydney
- Flooding in Somalia leaves hundreds homeless
- Orient Express ceases service
- United Arab Republic union dissolves
- Cyprus joins the Commonwealth of Nations

Super Bowl Champions Since You Were Born

These are the teams that have held a 7-pound, sterling silver Vince Lombardi trophy aloft during the Super Bowl era, and the number of times they've done it in your lifetime.

- **New England Patriots (6)**
  2001: The Super Bowl MVP, Tom Brady, had been a 6th round draft pick in 2000.
- Pittsburgh Steelers (6)
- Dallas Cowboys (5)
- San Francisco 49ers (5)
- **Green Bay Packers (4)**
  1967: To gain a berth in the Super Bowl, the Packers defeated the Dallas Cowboys in The Ice Bowl at 15 degrees below zero.
- New York Giants (4)
- **Denver Broncos (3)**
  2015: After the Broncos won their first Super Bowl 18 years prior, Broncos owner Pat Bowlen dedicated the victory to long-time quarterback John Elway ("This one's for John!"). After the 2015 victory, John Elway (now general manager) dedicated it to the ailing Bowlen ("This one's for Pat!").
- Washington Football Team (3)
- Las Vegas Raiders (3)
- Miami Dolphins (2)
- Indianapolis Colts (2)
- Kansas City Chiefs (2)
- Baltimore Ravens (2)
- Tampa Bay Buccaneers (2)
- **St. Louis/Los Angeles Rams (2)**
  1999: The Rams were led to the Super Bowl by Kurt Warner, who had been a grocery store clerk after college.
- Seattle Seahawks (1)
- Philadelphia Eagles (1)
- **Chicago Bears (1)**
  The 1985 Bears are known for their song, The Super Bowl Shuffle.
- New York Jets (1)
- New Orleans Saints (1)

Across the Nation

Voting. Joining the military. Turning 18 is serious stuff. Here's what everyone was reading about in the year you reached this milestone.

✦ Relations with Cuba severed
✦ Chimpanzee launched in Mercury capsule
✦ Peace Corp established
✦ Twenty-Third amendment passed
✦ Bay of Pigs invasion of Cuba fails
✦ Freedom riders take buses to the South
✦ Alan Shepherd launched into space
✦ President Kennedy vows to have a man on the moon by 1970
✦ Baseball All-Star Game ends in first ever tie
✦ Roger Maris beats Babe Ruth's one-season home run record
✦ Coca-Cola introduces Sprite
✦ Baseball's Ty Cobb died
✦ Vietnam War officially begins (right)
✦ Ernest Hemingway commits suicide
✦ Disposable diapers Pampers available
✦ Fake Morley cigarettes used in Psycho, and films since
✦ IBM Selectric Typewriter goes on sale
✦ First cordless electric toothbrush available
✦ TWA shows first inflight movie
  (By Love Possessed—shown in First Class)
✦ Fritos first sold by the newly created FritoLay company
✦ Barbie's boyfriend, Ken, makes an entrance
✦ Actor Gary Cooper died

Born this year:
  Barack Obama
  Actor George Clooney
  Actor Michael J. Fox
  Basketball player Dennis Rodman

Christmas 1961: nearly six years had passed since US army advisors were first posted to Vietnam. Troop numbers had swelled to over 3,000 alongside helicopters and planes; the first combat mission, Operation Chopper, was just weeks away.

US Open Champions

Winners while you were between the ages of the youngest (John McDermott, 1911, 19 years) and the oldest (Hale Irwin, 1990, at 45). Planning a win? Better hurry up!

1962	Jack Nicklaus
1963	Julius Boros
1964	Ken Venturi
1965	**Gary Player** First non-US winner of the US Open since 1925.
1966	Billy Casper
1967	Jack Nicklaus
1968	Lee Trevino
1969	Orville Moody
1970	Tony Jacklin
1971	Lee Trevino
1972	Jack Nicklaus
1973	**Johnny Miller** In 1973, 61-year-old Sam Snead became the oldest player ever to make the cut.
1974	Hale Irwin
1975	Lou Graham
1976	Jerry Pate
1977	Hubert Green
1978	Andy North
1979	Hale Irwin
1980	**Jack Nicklaus** Nicklaus set the record for years (18) between the first and last US Open victory.
1981	David Graham
1982	Tom Watson
1983	Larry Nelson
1984	Fuzzy Zoeller
1985	Andy North
1986	Raymond Floyd
1987	Scott Simpson
1988	Curtis Strange

Popular Girls' Names

If you started a family at a young age, these are the names you're most likely to have chosen. And even if you didn't pick them, a lot of Americans did!

Lisa
Lisa's second year in the top spot, having toppled Mary. Lisa would stay there until 1969 (when she was usurped by Jennifer).

Mary
Susan
Karen
Linda
Donna
Patricia
Lori
Sandra
Cynthia
Kimberly
Tammy
Deborah
Pamela
Brenda
Laura
Barbara
Teresa
Sharon
Elizabeth
Debra
Julie
Nancy
Cheryl
Robin
Michelle

Rising and falling stars:
Gina, Dana and Colleen graced the Top 100 for the first time; for Gloria, Shirley and Vicki it would be their last ever year in the spotlight.

Animals Extinct in Your Lifetime

Billions of passenger pigeons once flew the US skies. By 1914, they had been trapped to extinction. Not every species dies at our hands, but it's a sobering roll-call. (Date is year last known alive or declared extinct).

1943	Desert bandicoot
1945	Wake Island rail
1949	Sinu parakeet
1951	Yemen gazelle
1952	**Deepwater cisco fish** The deepwater cisco, once found in Lake Huron and Michigan, was overfished and crowded out by invasive parasites and alewife herring. Result? Extinction.
1952	San Benedicto rock wren
1960	Candango mouse, Brasilia
1962	Red-bellied opossum, Argentina
1963	Kākāwahie honeycreeper, Hawaii
1964	South Island snipe, New Zealand
1966	Arabian ostrich
1967	Saint Helena earwig
1967	**Yellow blossom pearly mussel** Habitat loss and pollution proved terminal for this Tennessee resident.
1971	Lake Pedder earthworm, Tasmania
1972	Bushwren, New Zealand
1981	Southern gastric-brooding frog, Australia
1986	Las Vegas dace
1989	Golden toad (see right)
1990	Dusky seaside sparrow, East Coast USA
2000	**Pyrenean ibex, Iberia** For a few minutes in 2003 this species was brought back to life through cloning, but sadly the newborn female ibex died.
2001	Caspian tiger, Central Asia
2012	**Pinta giant tortoise** The rarest creature in the world for the latter half of his 100-year life, Lonesome George of the Galapagos was the last remaining Pinta tortoise.

The observed history of the golden toad is brief and tragic. It wasn't discovered until 1964, abundant in a pristine area of Costa Rica. By 1989 it had gone, a victim of rising temperatures.

Popular Boys' Names

20

Here are the top boys' names for this year. Many of the most popular choices haven't shifted much since you were born, but more modern names are creeping in…

Michael
For 44 years from 1954 onwards, Michael was the nation's most popular name. (There was one blip in 1960 when David came first.)

John
David
James
Robert
Mark
William
Richard
Thomas
Jeffrey
Kevin
Scott
Joseph
Steven
Timothy
Charles
Paul
Kenneth
Daniel
Brian
Gregory
Anthony
Ronald
Gary
Donald
Christopher
Edward

Rising and falling stars:
Jim and Ralph ended their Top 100 run this year; Jose made his debut.

Popular Movies When You Were 21

The biggest stars in the biggest movies: these are the films the nation were enjoying as you entered into adulthood.

Dr. Strangelove Peter Sellers, George C. Scott, Sterling Hayden
Man's Favorite Sport? Rock Hudson, Paula Prentiss, Maria Perschy
Director Howard Hawks tried unsuccessfully to get Cary Grant and Katharine Hepburn to reprise their original roles in Bringing Up Baby.

Kissin' Cousins Elvis Presley, Arthur O'Connell, Glenda Farrell
The movie song reached #12 on the Billboard Hot 100.

Becket Richard Burton, Peter O'Toole, John Gielgud
The Pink Panther David Niven, Peter Sellers, Robert Wagner
From Russia With Love Sean Connery, Daniela Bianchi
The Carpetbaggers George Peppard, Alan Ladd, Bob Cummings
What a Way to Go! Shirley MacLaine, Paul Newman, Robert Mitchum
Viva Las Vegas Elvis Presley, Ann-Margret, Cesare Danova
A Shot in the Dark Peter Sellers, Elke Sommer, George Sanders
The Unsinkable Molly Brown Debbie Reynolds, Harve Presnell, Ed Begley
Good Neighbor Sam Jack Lemmon, Romy Schneider,
Marnie Tippi Hedren, Sean Connery, Diane Baker
A Hard Day's Night The Beatles
The Fall of the Roman Empire Sophia Loren, Stephen Boyd, Alec Guinness
Mary Poppins Julie Andrews, Dick Van Dyke, David Tomlinson
Topkapi Melina Mercouri, Maximilian Schell, Peter Ustinov
Send Me No Flowers Rock Hudson, Doris Day, Tony Randall
My Fair Lady Audrey Hepburn, Rex Harrison, Stanley Holloway
Roustabout Elvis Presley, Barbara Stanwyck, Joan Freeman
Father Goose Cary Grant, Leslie Caron, Trevor Howard
Goldfinger Sean Connery, Honor Blackman, Gert Frobe
Zorba the Greek Anthony Quinn, Alan Bates, Irene Papas
The Americanization of Emily Julie Andrews, James Garner, Melvyn Douglas

Across the Nation

21

A selection of national headlines from the year you turned 21. But how many can you remember?

- Martin Luther King Jr. selected Time's Man of the Year
- State lottery in New Hampshire begins
- G.I. Joe action figure bursts onto the scene
- Twenty-Fourth amendment ratified
- Rock'em Sock'em Robots introduced
- Pepsi Cola coins "the Pepsi generation"
- Mr. Whipple tells people to stop squeezing the Charmin
- Boston Strangler captured
- Ronald Reagan makes "A Time For Choosing" speech
- Civil Rights Act of 1964 passed
- World's Fair held in New York City
- Lyndon Johnson elected for president
- Sharpie marker introduced
- Malcolm X meets Martin Luther King Jr. (right)
- First political attack ad, "Daisy Girl," broadcast
- President Johnson declares "War on Poverty"
- Astronaut John Glenn runs for Senate
- Daisy Girl's target—Senator Barry Goldwater—runs for president
- Good Friday Earthquake strikes Alaska
- Draft cards are burned in protest
- Mississippi Burning: civil rights workers murdered
- Race riot on the streets of Philadelphia
- Warren Commission Report published
- Martin Luther King Jr. awarded Nobel Peace Prize

Born this year:
- Vice President Kamala Harris
- First Lady Michelle Obama
- Amazon founder Jeff Bezos
- Actress Courtney Cox

The only meeting between Martin Luther King and Malcolm X was a fleeting and unplanned encounter on Capitol Hill. Both were attending a hearing on a bill proposed by JFK—and now taken on by Lyndon Johnson—to end segregation. The differing approaches of these civil rights activists had kept them apart; Malcolm X had previously declined an invitation to meet. And although Malcolm X was in the crowd as King declared "I have a dream" at the 1963 March on Washington, to Malcom X the event had been a circus and a farce.

But in 1964, a meeting of minds seemed possible. Malcolm X had split from The Nation of Islam and told King that he was throwing himself "into the heart of the civil rights struggle." In 1965, while King was in jail, Malcolm X met Coretta Scott King and explained that he was there to encourage protesters to listen to her husband by showing "White people … what the alternative was." Two weeks later, Malcolm X was assassinated.

The Biggest Hits When You Were 21

The artists you love at 21 are with you for life. How many of these hits from this milestone year can you still hum or sing in the tub?

Martha and the Vandellas ♪ Dancing in the Street
The Drifters ♪ Under the Boardwalk
Manfred Mann ♪ Do Wah Diddy Diddy
The Animals ♪ Boom Boom
Mary Wells ♪ My Guy
The Beatles ♪ She Loves You
Louis Armstrong ♪ Hello, Dolly!
Jim Reeves ♪ I Won't Forget You
The Supremes ♪ Where Did Our Love Go
The Animals ♪ House of the Rising Sun
Roy Orbison ♪ Oh, Pretty Woman
The Righteous Brothers ♪ You've Lost That Loving Feeling
Stan Getz and Joao Gilberto ♪ The Girl from Ipanema
The Shangri-Las ♪ Leader of the Pack
The Dave Clark Five ♪ Glad All Over
The Four Tops ♪ Baby I Need Your Loving
Leslie Gore ♪ You Don't Own Me
The Beatles ♪ I Feel Fine
Jay and the Americans ♪ Come a Little Bit Closer
Dionne Warwick ♪ Walk On By
Chuck Berry ♪ No Particular Place to Go
Junior Walker and the All Stars ♪ Shotgun
The Temptations ♪ The Way You Do
the Things You Do
The Beach Boys ♪ Fun, Fun, Fun

Popular Food in the 1960s

Changes in society didn't stop at the front door: a revolution in the kitchen brought us exotic new recipes, convenience in a can, and even space-age fruit flavors. These are the tastes of a decade, but how many of them were on the menu for your family?

McDonald's Big Mac
First served in 1967 by a Pittsburgh franchisee.

Royal Shake-a-Pudd'n Dessert Mix

Tunnel of Fudge Cake

Campbell's SpaghettiOs

Pop-Tarts

B&M's canned bread

Cool Whip
A time-saving delight that originally contained no milk or cream, meaning that it could be frozen and transported easily.

Grasshopper pie

Beech-Nut Fruit Stripe Gum

Sandwich Loaf

Lipton Onion Soup Dip
Millions of packets are still sold each year of this favorite that was once known as "Californian Dip".

Jello salad

Hires Root Beer

Baked Alaska

Tang
Invented by William A. Mitchell who also concocted Cool Whip, Tang was used by astronauts to flavor the otherwise unpalatable water on board the Gemini and Apollo missions.

Corn Diggers

Teem soda

Eggo Waffles

Kraft Shake 'N Bake

Maypo oatmeal
In 1985, Dire Straights sang, "I want my MTV"—an echo of the stars who'd shouted the same words to promote the new station. But 30 years before that (and the inspiration for MTV's campaign), an animated child yelled, "I want my Maypo!"

Fashion in the Sixties

As a child, you (generally) wear what you're given. It's only in hindsight, on fading Polaroids, that you recognize that your outfits carried the fashion imprint of the day. Whether you were old or bold enough to carry off a pair of bell bottoms, though, is a secret that should remain between you and your photo albums.

Bell bottoms
Bell bottoms were widely available at Navy surplus and thrift stores at a time when second-hand shopping was on the rise.

Miniskirts and mini dresses

Peasant blouses

Rudi Gernreich
Pope Paul IV banned Catholics from wearing his monokini—a topless swim suit.

US flag clothing

Tulle turbans

Shift dresses

Collarless jackets
This jacket trend was popularized by the Beatles in 1963.

Babydoll dresses

V-neck tennis sweaters

Afghan coats

Leopard print clothing
In 1962, Jackie Kennedy wore a leopard print coat which caused a spike in demand for leopard skin, leading to the death of up to 250,000 leopards. The coat's designer, Oleg Cassini, felt guilty about it for the rest of his life.

Tie-dye clothing

Short, brightly colored, shapeless dresses

Pillbox hats

Mary Quant

Maxi skirts

Bonnie Cashin

Plaid

Poor boy sweaters

Pea coats

Around the World When You Turned 25

With the growing reach of news organizations, events from outside our borders were sometimes front-page news. How many do you remember?

✦ Liberal reforms in Czechoslovakia temporarily result in the Prague Spring
✦ Soviets and allies crush Czechoslovakia
✦ Polish authorities brutally squash student marches
✦ Vietnam War protests occur worldwide
✦ Winter Olympics open in France
✦ Soviet module orbits moon, returns successfully
✦ Businessman buys London Bridge
✦ Pope Paul VI bans Catholics from using birth control pill
✦ Earthquake rocks Sicily
✦ Equatorial Guinea gains independence
✦ Hong Kong flu pandemic kills 1 million worldwide
✦ Students protest in Mexico City
✦ Aswan Dam is completed in Egypt
✦ Protestors in Brazil march against military dictatorship
✦ Volcano in Costa Rica erupts after centuries of dormancy
✦ Australian prime minister disappears
✦ Ferry sinks in New Zealand
✦ Olympics open in Mexico City
✦ Buenos Aires football riot kills 74
✦ Workers and students riot in Paris
✦ Earthquake and tsunami hit the Philippines
✦ English yachtsman sails around the world in 354 days
✦ China celebrates 20 years of rule under Mao
✦ Canada elects Pierre Trudeau as PM
✦ Revolution ends in Peru

Cars of the 1960s

Smaller cars. More powerful cars. More distinctive cars. More variety, yes: but the success of imported models such as the Volkswagen Beetle was a sign that more fundamental changes lay ahead for The Big Three.

1940	Ford Lincoln Continental
1949	Volkswagen Beetle
1950	Volkswagen Type 2 (Microbus)
1958	**General Motors Chevrolet Impala**
	In 1965, the Impala sold more than 1 million units, the most sold by any model in the US since WWII.
1958	American Motors Corporation Rambler Ambassador
1959	General Motors Chevrolet El Camino
1959	Ford Galaxie
1960	**Ford Falcon**
	The cartoon strip "Peanuts" was animated for TV to market the Falcon.
1960	General Motors Pontiac Tempest
1960	General Motors Chevrolet Corvair
1961	**Jaguar E-Type**
	Ranked first in The Daily Telegraph UK's list of the world's "100 most beautiful cars" of all time.
1961	Chrysler Newport
1962	Shelby Cobra
1963	General Motors Buick Riviera
1963	Porsche 911
1963	Kaiser-Jeep Jeep Wagoneer
1964	**Ford Mustang**
	The song of the same name reached #6 on the R&B Charts in 1966. That year, more Ford Mustangs were sold (550,000) than any other car.
1964	General Motors Chevrolet Chevelle
1964	Chrysler Plymouth Barracuda
1964	General Motors Pontiac GTO
1967	General Motors Chevrolet Camaro
1967	Ford Mercury Cougar
1968	Chrysler Plymouth Road Runner

Books of the Decade

Were you a voracious bookworm in your twenties? Or a more reluctant reader, only drawn by the biggest titles of the day? Here are the new titles that fought for your attention.

1963	The Bell Jar by Sylvia Plath
1963	The Feminine Mystique by Betty Friedan
1963	A Clockwork Orange by Anthony Burgess
1964	The Group by Mary McCarthy
1964	Herzog by Saul Bellow
1964	The Spy Who Came in from the Cold by John le Carré
1964	Up the Down Staircase by Bel Kaufman
1965	Dune by Frank Herbert
1966	Valley of the Dolls by Jacqueline Susann
1966	In Cold Blood by Truman Capote
1967	Rosemary's Baby by Ira Levin
1967	The Arrangement by Elia Kazan
1967	The Confessions of Nat Turner by William Styron
1968	Airport by Arthur Hailey
1968	Couples by John Updike
1969	The Godfather by Mario Puzo
1969	Slaughterhouse-Five by Kurt Vonnegut
1969	Portnoy's Complaint by Philip Roth
1969	The French Lieutenant's Woman by John Fowles
1970	Love Story by Erich Segal
1970	One Hundred Years of Solitude by Gabriel Garcia Marquez
1971	The Happy Hooker: My Own Story by Xaviera Hollander
1971	The Exorcist by William Peter Blatty
1972	Watership Down by Richard Adams
1972	The Joy of Sex by Alex Comfort
1972	Fear and Loathing in Las Vegas by Hunter S. Thompson

Prominent Americans

This new set of definitive stamps, issued from 1965 onwards, aimed to do a better job of capturing the diversity of the Americans who made a nation. The series doubled the previous number of women depicted...to two. How many did you have in your collection?

Thomas Jefferson 1 ¢ 🖼 Third US President
Albert Gallatin 1 ¼ ¢ 🖼 Fourth Treasury Secretary
Frank Lloyd Wright 2 ¢ 🖼 Architect
Francis Parkman 3 ¢ 🖼 Historian
Abraham Lincoln 4 ¢ 🖼 16th US President
George Washington 5 ¢ 🖼 First US President
Franklin D Roosevelt 6 ¢ 🖼 32nd US President
Dwight Eisenhower 6 / 8 ¢ 🖼 34th US President
In 1957, Eisenhower became the first president to travel by helicopter instead of a limo, en route to Camp David (which he had called Shangri-La, but renamed after his grandson).

Benjamin Franklin 7 ¢ 🖼 Polymath
Albert Einstein 8 ¢ 🖼 Physicist
Andrew Jackson 10 ¢ 🖼 7th US President
Henry Ford 12 ¢ 🖼 Founder of Ford Motor Company
John F. Kennedy 13 ¢ 🖼 35th US President
Fiorello LaGuardia 14 ¢ 🖼 Mayor of New York City in WWII
Read Dick Tracy comics on the radio during a paper strike.

Oliver Wendell Holmes, Jr 15 ¢ 🖼 Supreme Court Justice
Ernie Pyle 16 ¢ 🖼 Journalist during World War II
Elizabeth Blackwell 18 ¢ 🖼 First woman to get a medical degree.
After 11 college rejections, male students at Geneva Medical College all voted for her acceptance. They did it as a joke.

George C Marshall 20 ¢ 🖼 Sec. of State and Sec. of Defense
Amadeo Giannini 21 ¢ 🖼 Founder of Bank of America
Frederick Douglass 25 ¢ 🖼 Slavery escapee, abolitionist leader
John Dewey 30 ¢ 🖼 Educational pioneer
Thomas Paine 40 ¢ 🖼 Helped inspire the American Revolution
Lucy Stone 50 ¢ 🖼 Suffragist and slavery campaigner
Eugene O'Neill $1 🖼 Playwright
John Bassett Moore $5 🖼 Jurist

Sixties Game Shows

Recovery from the quiz show scandal of the fifties was a gradual process. Big prize money was out; games were in—the sillier the better, or centered around relationships. "Popcorn for the mind," as game show creator Chuck Barris memorably put it.

College Bowl 🎥 (1953–70)

Snap Judgment 🏆 (1967–69)

To Tell The Truth 🎥 (1956–present)

Dough Re Mi 🎥 (1958–60)

Camouflage 🏆 (1961–62 & 1980)

Dream House 🎥 (1968–84)

Say When!! 🏆 (1961–65)

Let's Make A Deal 🎥 (1963–present)
The long-time presenter of the show, Monty Hall, gave rise to the eponymous problem: when one door in three hides a prize and you've made your pick, should you change your answer when the host reveals a "zonk" (dud) behind another door? (The counterintuitive answer is yes!)

Your First Impression 🎥 (1962–64)

Supermarket Sweep 🎥 (1965–present)
In one of its many comebacks, 1990 episodes of Supermarket Sweep featured monsters roaming the aisles including Frankenstein and Mr. Yuk.

You Don't Say! 🎥 1963–79)

It's Your Bet 🎥 (1969–73)

Yours For A Song 🏆 (1961–63)

Concentration 🎥 (1958–91)

Seven Keys 🏆 (1960–65)

Queen For A Day 🎥 1945–1970)

Password 🎥 (1961–75)

Video Village 🎥 (1960–62)

Who Do You Trust? 🏆 (1957–63)
Originally titled, "Do You Trust Your Wife?"

Personality 🏆 (1967–69)

Beat The Odds 🏆 (1961–69)

Across the Nation

30

Another decade passes and you're well into adulthood. Were you reading the news, or making it? Here are the national stories that dominated the front pages.

- Last ground troops leave Vietnam
- Supreme Court decides Roe v. Wade
- Vice President Spiro Agnew resigns
- President Richard Nixon makes "I'm not a crook" speech
- Gerald Ford selected as Vice President
- Cell phone call made between research rivals
- Congress authorizes Bicentennial coin designs
- Secretariat becomes Triple Crown winner
- Burger King decides to let customers have it their way
- Major car plants close
- Watergate hearings begin
- Skylab launched
- Billie Jean King defeats Bobby Riggs in tennis match
- Saturday Night Massacre leads to demands for impeachment
- Nixon accepts resignations of Watergate conspirators
- Miami Dolphins play undefeated season to Super Bowl
- President Lyndon Johnson died
- Oakland A's win the World Series
- Endangered Species Act signed
- American Indian Movement occupy Wounded Knee (right)
- John McCain among those prisoners released by Vietnam
- Army begins All Volunteer Force program
- President releases tapes connected to Watergate scandal
- Henry Kissinger sworn in as Secretary of State

Born this year:
- Singer Pharrell Williams
- Google cofounder Larry Page
- TV host Seth Meyers

Dennis Banks, cofounder of the American Indian Movement (AIM), addresses the crowd during the occupation of Wounded Knee, site of the 1890 massacre. The 1973 siege lasted 71 days; two died, one disappeared, and the town was destroyed.

The Biggest Hits When You Were 30...

How many of these big tunes from the year you turned thirty will still strike a chord decades later?

Steely Dan ♪ Do It Again

Stevie Wonder ♪ Higher Ground

Gladys Knight and the Pips ♪ Midnight Train to Georgia

Elton John ♪ Crocodile Rock

Marvin Gaye ♪ Let's Get It On

Ringo Starr ♪ Photograph

The Rolling Stones ♪ Angie

Stealers Wheel ♪ Stuck in the Middle with You

Jim Croce ♪ Bad, Bad Leroy Brown

Deep Purple ♪ Smoke on the Water

The O'Jays ♪ Love Train

Roberta Flack ♪ Killing Me Softly with His Words

Pink Floyd ♪ Money

The Four Tops ♪ Ain't No Woman
(Like the One I've Got)

Carly Simon ♪ You're So Vain

Charlie Rich ♪ The Most Beautiful Girl

Tony Orlando and Dawn ♪ Tie a Yellow Ribbon
Round the Ole Oak Tree

Anne Murray ♪ A Love Song

The Sweet ♪ Ballroom Blitz

Dobie Gray ♪ Drift Away

Stevie Wonder ♪ You Are the Sunshine of My Life

Lou Reed ♪ Walk on the Wild Side

George Harrison ♪ Give Me Love
(Give Me Peace on Earth)

The Spinners ♪ Could It Be I'm Falling In Love

...and the Movies You Saw That Year, Too

From award winners to crowd pleasers, here are the movies that played as your third decade drew to a close.

Westworld	Yul Brynner, Richard Benjamin, James Brolin
Jesus Christ Superstar	Ted Neeley, Carl Anderson, Yvonne Elliman
Jonathan Livingston Seagull	James Franciscus, Juliet Mills, Hal Holbrook
The Lost Horizon	Peter Finch, Liv Ullmann, Sally Kellerman
Paper Moon	Ryan O'Neal, Madeline Kahn, John Hillerman
The Way We Were	Barbra Streisand, Robert Redford
The Sting	Paul Newman, Robert Redford, Robert Shaw
The Day of the Jackal	Edward Fox, Michael Lonsdale, Terence Alexander
American Graffiti	Richard Dreyfuss, Ron Howard, Paul Le Mat
High Plains Drifter	Verna Bloom, Billy Curtis, Buddy Van Horn
The Day of the Dolphin	George C. Scott, Trish Van Devere, Paul Sorvino
A Touch of Class	George Segal, Glenda Jackson, Paul Sorvino

Cary Grant and Roger Moore both turned down chances to be the lead.

Papillon	Steve McQueen, Dustin Hoffman, Victory Jory
The World's Greatest Athlete	John Amos, Roscoe Lee Browne, Tim Conway
Sleeper	Woody Allen, Diane Keaton, John Beck
Pat Garrett and Billy the Kid	James Coburn, Kris Kristofferson, Richard Jaeckel
Robin Hood	Brian Bedford, Roger Miller, Monica Evans
Serpico	Al Pacino, John Randolph, Jack Kehoe
Battle for the Planet of the Apes	Roddy McDowell, Claude Akins, Natalie Trundy
Live and Let Die	Roger Moore, Yaphet Kotto, Jane Seymour
Magnum Force	Clint Eastwood, Hal Holbrook, Mitchell Ryan
Enter the Dragon	Jim Kelly, John Saxon, Ahna Capri
The Exorcist	Ellen Burstyn, Max von Sydow, Linda Blair
The Last Detail	Jack Nicholson, Otis Young, Randy Quaid

Around the House

Sometimes with a fanfare but often by stealth, inventions and innovations transformed the 20th-century household. Here's what arrived between the ages of 10 and 30.

1953	**WD-40 spray** Now a household essential, "Water Displacement 40th Formula" was created for the aerospace industry to protect, clean, and lubricate—much as it is now used by everyone else.
1955	TV remote control
1956	Snooze alarm clock
1956	Velcro
1957	First electric watch
1959	Princess line telephone
1961	Head & Shoulders shampoo
1962	Arco lamp
1963	**Chips Ahoy! chocolate chip cookies** An elementary teacher and her class wrote Nabisco saying that they did not find 1000 chips in the bag of Chips Ahoy, though the bag clearly states it has that many. Nabisco flew a representative to their school and demonstrated to the students (and the media) how to actually find all the chips.
1963	Push button Touchtone phone
1964	Portable TVs
1964	Sharpie permanent markers
1965	Cordless telephone
1967	Close-up toothpaste
1968	Bean bag chair
1970	**Irish Spring soap** Irish Spring soap's catchy tune and tag lines became part of the language with "Clean as a whistle" and "I like it too!" While it generated a lot of bad Irish accents, it has nothing to do with Ireland.
1971	Soft contact lenses
1972	Science calculator

Here's one that didn't quite make the grade: AT&T's Picturephone, demonstrated here at the 1964 New York World's Fair. A trial set up that year invited the public to rent two of the Picturephone rooms set up in New York, Chicago, and Washington ($16 for 3 minutes). The take-up over the following years was almost nil, but Picturephones went on sale in 1970 anyway with a prediction of a billion-dollar business by 1980. The devices

Female Olympic Gold Medalists in Your Lifetime

These are the women who have stood atop the podium the greatest number of times at the Summer Olympics, whether in individual or team events.

Jenny Thompson (8) ⚭ Swimming
Thompson is an anesthesiologist. She started her medical training in 2000—although she took time out while studying to win further gold World Championship medals.

Katie Ledecky (7) ⚭ Swimming
Allyson Felix (7) ⚭ Athletics
Amy Van Dyken (6) ⚭ Swimming
Dana Vollmer (5) ⚭ Swimming
Missy Franklin (5) ⚭ Swimming
Sue Bird (5) ⚭ Basketball
Diana Taurasi (5) ⚭ Basketball
The late Kobe Bryant dubbed Taurasi the "white mamba"; for others she is the G.O.A.T. in women's basketball.

Allison Schmitt (4) ⚭ Swimming
Dara Torres (4) ⚭ Swimming
Evelyn Ashford (4) ⚭ Athletics
Janet Evans (4) ⚭ Swimming
Lisa Leslie (4) ⚭ Basketball
Pat McCormick (4) ⚭ Diving
Sanya Richards-Ross (4) ⚭ Athletics
Serena Williams (4) ⚭ Tennis
Simone Biles (4) ⚭ Gymnastics
Biles's phenomenal medal tally in Olympics and World Championships is greater than any other US gymnast.

Tamika Catchings (4) ⚭ Basketball
Teresa Edwards (4) ⚭ Basketball
Venus Williams (4) ⚭ Tennis

Around the World When You Turned 35

It's a big news day every day, somewhere in the world. Here are the stories that the media thought you'd want to read in the year of your 35th birthday.

- ✦ Israel and Egypt sign peace accords
- ✦ Iran earthquake kills 20,000
- ✦ Solo explorer reaches North Pole
- ✦ Chaplin's remains are stolen
- ✦ Rhodesia attacks Zambia
- ✦ Test-tube baby born
- ✦ Dominica gains independence
- ✦ Israel invades Lebanon
- ✦ Spain establishes new constitution
- ✦ Terrorists explode bomb in Versailles
- ✦ Sweden bans aerosol sprays
- ✦ Three Popes reign during the year
- ✦ Monsoons leave millions homeless in India
- ✦ Argentina wins World Cup
- ✦ Oil tanker crash causes disaster in Brittany
- ✦ Assassin uses umbrella to kill defector
- ✦ Jonestown massacre takes place
- ✦ Botha becomes South Africa PM
- ✦ Nobel peace prize is given to Sadat and Begin
- ✦ Powerful earthquake hits Greece
- ✦ Soviets shoot down Korean airliner
- ✦ Afghan Civil War begins
- ✦ Iranian helicopters shot down in Soviet airspace
- ✦ Military coup fails in Ethiopia
- ✦ Remains of pyramid is uncovered in Mexico City

Drinks of the Sixties

For many of those slipping from adolescence into adulthood, your choice of drink says a lot about you. Sophisticated or down-to-earth? A classic, or something to make a statement? In the years that follow, the drinks might change, but the decision remains the same! Here's what was behind a sixties bar.

Falstaff beer

Rusty Nail cocktail
Rumored to be a favorite drink of the Rat Pack.

Hull's Cream Ale
Stinger cocktail
Rheingold Extra Dry Lager
Gunther's Beer
Lone Star Beer
The Gimlet cocktail
The Grasshopper cocktail

Little King's Cream Ale
Best known for its miniature seven-ounce bottles.

Mai Thai cocktail
Genesee Cream Ale

Storz Beer
From Nebraska, Storz was "Brewed for the beer pro."

Iron City Beer
Iron City is reputed to have introduced the first twist-off bottle cap in 1963.

Golden Dream cocktail

Mint Julep cocktail
It's the official drink of the Kentucky Derby, with around 120,000 served over the weekend.

Koch's Light Lager Beer
Arrow 77 Beer
Daiquiri cocktail
Manhattan cocktail
Sterling Premium Pilsner
Carling Black Label
Hamm's Beer
Old fashioned cocktail

Seventies Game Shows

With enough water under the bridge since the 1950s scandals, producers of seventies game shows injected big money into new formats and revamped favorites, some of them screened five nights a week. How many did you cheer on from the couch?

High Rollers 🏆 (1974-88)

Gambit 🏆 (1972-81)

The New Treasure Hunt 🏆 (1973-82)
Perhaps the best-known episode of this show saw a woman faint when she won a Rolls Royce—that she later had to sell in order to pay the taxes.

The Cross-Wits 🏆 (1975-87)

Hollywood Squares 🏆 1966-2004)

The Newlywed Game 🏆 (1966-2013)
Show creator Chuck Barris also made "3's a Crowd"— the show in which men, their secretaries and their wives competed. The public wasn't happy.

Pyramid 🏆 (1973-present)
Thanks to inflation and rival prizes, the $10,000 Pyramid in 1973 didn't last long: from 1976 it was raised in increments to its current peak of $100,000.

Dealer's Choice 🏆 (1974-75)

Sports Challenge 🏆 (1971-79)

Tattletales 🏆 (1974-84)

It's Your Bet 🏆 (1969-73)

Celebrity Sweepstakes 🏆 (1974-77)

Rhyme and Reason 🏆 (1975-76)

Three On A Match 🏆 (1971-74)

The Match Game 🏆 (1962-present)

Sale of the Century 🏆 (1969-89)

The Dating Game 🏆 (1965-99)
The Dating Game—known as Blind Date in many international versions—saw many celebrity appearances before they became well-known, including the Carpenters and Arnold Schwarzenegger.

Popular Boys' Names

Just as middle age crept up unnoticed, so the most popular names also evolved. The traditional choices—possibly including yours—are fast losing their appeal to new parents.

Michael
Christopher
Matthew
David
Joshua
James
Jason
Daniel
John
Robert
Joseph
Justin
Ryan
Brian
Andrew
William
Brandon
Adam
Having entered the Top 100 in 1970, this was Adam's high point to date (though he still ranks in the lower reaches).

Jonathan
Eric
Nicholas
Anthony
Steven
Thomas
Kevin
Timothy
Rising and falling stars:
1983 was a very quiet year in names: only Evan joined, and nobody left the Top 100 for good.

Popular Girls' Names

40

It's a similar story for girls' names. Increasing numbers are taking their infant inspiration from popular culture. The worlds of music, film and theater are all fertile hunting grounds for those in need of inspiration.

Jennifer
Jessica
Amanda
Ashley
Sarah
Melissa
Nicole
Stephanie
Heather
Elizabeth
A name's moment in the sun spans years, sometimes decades. But eventually they disappear out of sight... unless you're Elizabeth. For over a century she's floated between 6th and 26th position.

Crystal
Amy
Michelle
Tiffany
Kimberly
Christina
Amber
Erin
Rebecca
Rachel
Megan
Angela
Laura
Lauren
Rising and falling stars:
Girls we welcomed for the first time this year: Meghan, Kayla, Bethany and—for one year only—Desiree. Names we'd never see in the Top 100 again: Pamela, Heidi, Renee, Jill and Tina.

NBA Champions
Since You Were Born

These are the winners of the NBA Finals in your lifetime—
and the number of times they've taken the title.

- Philadelphia Warriors (2)
- Baltimore Bullets (1)
- Minneapolis Lakers (5)
- Rochester Royals (1)
- Syracuse Nationals (1)
- **Boston Celtics (17)**
  1966: After the Lakers won Game 1 of the NBA Finals, the Celtics named their star Bill Russell player-coach. He was the first black coach in the NBA. The Celtics responded by winning the series.

- St. Louis Hawks (1)
- Philadelphia 76ers (2)
- New York Knicks (2)
- Milwaukee Bucks (2)
- **Los Angeles Lakers (12)**
  1980: With Kareem Abdul-Jabbar out with an injury, Lakers' 20-year-old rookie Magic Johnson started at center in the clinching Game 6 and scored 42 points and snared 15 rebounds.

- **Golden State Warriors (5)**
  2015: LeBron James and Stephen Curry, the stars of the teams that faced off in the 2015 NBA Finals, were both born in the same hospital in Akron, Ohio.

- Portland Trail Blazers (1)
- Washington Bullets (1)
- Seattle SuperSonics (1)
- Detroit Pistons (3)
- Chicago Bulls (6)
- Houston Rockets (2)
- San Antonio Spurs (5)
- Miami Heat (3)
- Dallas Mavericks (1)
- Cleveland Cavaliers (1)
- Toronto Raptors (1)

Fashion in the Seventies

The decade that taste forgot? Or a kickback against the sixties and an explosion of individuality? Skirts got shorter (and longer). Block colors and peasant chic vied with sequins and disco glamor. How many of your seventies outfits would you still wear today?

Wrap dresses
Diane von Fürstenberg said she invented the silent, no-zipper wrap dress for one-night stands. "Haven't you ever tried to creep out of the room unnoticed the following morning? I've done that many times."

Tube tops
Midi skirt
In 1970, fashion designers began to lower the hemlines on the mini skirt. This change wasn't welcomed by many consumers. Women picketed in New York City with "stop the midi" signs.

Track suit, running shoes, soccer jerseys
Cowl neck sweaters
His & hers matching outfits
Cork-soled platform shoes
Caftans, Kaftans, Kimonos and mummus
Prairie dresses
Cuban heels
Gaucho pants
Chokers and dog collars as necklaces
Birkenstocks
Tennis headbands
Turtleneck shirts
Puffer vests
Long knit vests layered over tops and pants
Military surplus rucksack bags
"Daisy Dukes" denim shorts
Daisy's revealing cut-off denim shorts in The Dukes of Hazzard caught the attention of network censors. The answer for actor Catherine Bach? Wear flesh-colored pantyhose–just in case.

Yves Saint Laurent
Shrink tops
Bill Gibb

Drinks of the Seventies

Breweries were bigger, and there were fewer of them. Beers were lighter. But what could you (or your parents) serve with your seventies fondue? How about a cocktail that's as heavy on the double-entendre as it was on the sloe gin? Or perhaps match the decade's disco theme with a splash of blue curaçao?

Amber Moon cocktail
Features an unbroken, raw egg and featured in the film Murder on the Orient Express.

Billy Beer
Rainier Beer
Point Special Lager
Tequila Sunrise cocktail
Regal Select Light Beer
Stroh's rum
Long Island Iced Tea cocktail
Merry Widow cocktail
Shell's City Pilsner Premium Beer
Brass Monkey cocktail
The Godfather cocktail
Brown Derby
Sea-Breeze cocktail

Schlitz
This Milwaukee brewery was the country's largest in the late sixties and early seventies. But production problems were followed by a disastrous ad campaign, and by 1981 the original brewery was closed.

Alabama Slammer cocktail
Golden Cadillac cocktail
Harvey Wallbanger cocktail
Red White & Blue Special Lager Beer
Lite Beer from Miller

Coors Banquet Beer
A beer that made the most of its initial limited distribution network by floating the idea of contraband Coors. The idea was so successful that Coors smuggling became central to the plot of the movie Smokey and the Bandit.

US Open Tennis

Across the Open Era and the US National Championship that preceded it, these men won between the year you turned 19 (matching the youngest ever champ, Pete Sampras) and 38 (William Larned's age with his seventh win, in 1911).

1962	Rod Laver
1963	Rafael Osuna
1964	Roy Emerson
1965	Manuel Santana
1966	Fred Stolle
1967	**John Newcombe**

Newcombe was George W. Bush's drinking companion the day in 1976 when Bush was charged with driving under the influence of alcohol.

1968	Arthur Ashe
1969	Rod Laver
1970	Ken Rosewall
1971	Stan Smith
1972	Illie Nastase
1973	John Newcombe
1974	Jimmy Connors
1975	**Manuel Orantes**

Orantes came back from 5-0 down in the 4th set of the semifinal to win the 4th and 5th sets and upset top-seeded Jimmy Connors in the final.

1976	Jimmy Connors
1977	Guillermo Vilas
1978	**Jimmy Connors**

Connors became the only player to win on all three surfaces that have been used by the US Open.

1979–81	John McEnroe

Books of the Decade

Family, friends, TV, and more: there are as many midlife distractions as there are books on the shelf. Did you get drawn in by these bestsellers, all published in your thirties?

1973	Fear of Flying by Erica Jong
1973	Gravity's Rainbow by Thomas Pynchon
1974	Jaws by Peter Benchley
1974	The Front Runner by Patricia Nell Warren
1975	The Eagle Has Landed by Jack Higgins
1975	Shōgun by James Clavell
1975	Ragtime by E.L. Doctorow
1976	Roots by Alex Haley
1976	The Hite Report by Shere Hite
1977	The Thorn Birds by Colleen McCullough
1977	The Women's Room by Marilyn French
1978	Eye of the Needle by Ken Follett
1978	The World According to Garp by John Irving
1979	Flowers in the Attic by V.C. Andrews
1979	The Hitchhiker's Guide to the Galaxy by Douglas Adams
1979	Sophie's Choice by William Styron
1980	Rage of Angels by Sidney Sheldon
1980	The Bourne Identity by Robert Ludlum
1980	The Covenant by James Michener
1981	The Hotel New Hampshire by John Irving
1981	Noble House by James Clavell
1981	An Indecent Obsession by Colleen McCullough
1982	The Color Purple by Alice Walker
1982	Space by James A. Michener

Around the World When You Turned 40

International stories from farflung places—but did they appear on your radar as you clocked up four decades on the planet?

- ✦ Zimbabwe civil war begins
- ✦ Gold bars are stolen at Heathrow airport
- ✦ 38 prisoners break out of Irish high-security Maze prison
- ✦ UK makes seat belts mandatory
- ✦ IRA explodes bomb outside Harrods
- ✦ Ethiopia pleads for help as famine worsens
- ✦ Benigno Aquino is assassinated in the Philippines
- ✦ Thatcher wins landslide victory as prime minister
- ✦ Nazi Klaus Barbie is arrested
- ✦ Theater fire in Turin kills 62
- ✦ Bushfires in Australia kill 75
- ✦ Muslims are murdered in India during Nellie massacre
- ✦ Car bomb in South Africa kills 19
- ✦ Powerful earthquake strikes Japan
- ✦ Poland ends martial law
- ✦ Civil war begins in Sri Lanka
- ✦ Terrible flooding devastates Spain
- ✦ Soviet jet shoots down Korean airliner
- ✦ Soyuz mission aborted after launch pad fire
- ✦ Australian yacht wins the America's Cup
- ✦ Coup in Grenada overthrows government
- ✦ Argentina holds democratic elections
- ✦ Soviets misinterpret NATO maneuvers as nuclear first strike
- ✦ Killer in UK is identified using DNA
- ✦ Two bombs explode in Paris

Across the Nation

Here are the headline stories from across the country in the year you hit 40.

- ✦ Texas coast hit by Hurricane Alicia
- ✦ Invasion of Grenada is launched (right)
- ✦ Sally Ride becomes the first woman to walk in space
- ✦ Strategic Defense Initiative (SDI) proposed
- ✦ Best Buy and Papa John's got their starts
- ✦ Earthquake hits New York
- ✦ Land speed record of 633.468 mph set in Nevada
- ✦ Truck bomb hits Marine barracks in Beirut
- ✦ Motorola releases mobile phone
- ✦ Cabbage Patch dolls go on sale
- ✦ ARPANET changes to use Internet protocols, creating the Internet
- ✦ Microsoft Word released
- ✦ IBM PC XT released
- ✦ Barney Frank dies 112 days after his artificial heart implanted
- ✦ Robbery of a gambling club in Seattle leaves 13 dead
- ✦ Vanessa Williams crowned Miss America
- ✦ Martin Luther King Day signed into law
- ✦ McNuggets are on the menu
- ✦ Washington Redskins win the Super Bowl
- ✦ Baltimore Orioles win the World Series
- ✦ Space Shuttle Challenger makes maiden flight
- ✦ Compact discs become available
- ✦ Apple IIe goes on sale
- ✦ Consumer camcorders released to the public

Born this year:

- ⚭ Actor Donald Glover
- ⚭ NSA whistleblower Edward Snowden
- ⚭ Actor Aziz Ansari

The invasion of the small Caribbean island nation of Grenada began at dawn on October 25, 1983. Codenamed Operation Urgent Fury, the order to restore stability and safeguard around 600 US students and holidaymakers, took US Army planners by surprise. Many had been expecting a mission to the Middle East, where 241 US marines had recently lost their lives in a truck bomb attack. Instead they improvised with tourist maps, and the island assault quickly overthrew the unstable military government and installed an interim administration. Although criticized internationally, the action was deemed "a complete success" by the commander in charge, Admiral McDonald (above).

The Biggest Hits When You Were 40

Big tunes for a big birthday: how many of them enticed your middle-aged party guests onto the dance floor?

Duran Duran ♪ Hungry Like the Wolf
Marvin Gaye ♪ Sexual Healing
The Police ♪ Every Breath You Take
Michael Jackson ♪ Billie Jean
Prince ♪ 1999
Kenny Rogers
and Dolly Parton ♪ Islands in the Stream
Bryan Adams ♪ This Time
New Edition ♪ Candy Girl
Yes ♪ Owner of a Lonely Heart
Stevie Ray Vaughan ♪ Pride and Joy
B.J. Thomas ♪ What Ever Happened To
Old Fashioned Love
Michael Jackson ♪ Beat It
The S.O.S. Band ♪ Just Be Good To Me
Madonna ♪ Holiday
John Anderson ♪ Swingin'
Culture Club ♪ Karma Chameleon
Kenny Rogers
and Sheena Easton ♪ We've Got Tonight
Rufus and Chaka Khan ♪ Ain't Nobody
David Bowie ♪ Let's Dance
Def Leppard ♪ Rock of Ages
Irene Cara ♪ Flashdance... What a Feeling
Michael Jackson
and Paul McCartney ♪ Say Say Say
Men Without Hats ♪ Safety Dance
Mtume ♪ Juicy Fruit

Popular Food in the 1970s

From fads to ads, here's a new collection of dinner party dishes and family favorites. This time it's the seventies that's serving up the delights—and some of us are still enjoying them today!

Watergate Salad
Black Forest cake
Chex Mix
Cheese Tid-Bits
Dolly Madison Koo-koos (cupcakes)

Life Cereal
"I'm not gonna try it. You try it. Let's get Mikey…he hates everything." Three on- and off-screen brothers, one memorable ad that ran for much of the seventies.

The Manwich
"A sandwich is a sandwich, but a manwich is a meal," the ads announced in 1969.

Tomato aspic
Bacardi rum cake
Impossible pies
Zucchini bread
Oscar Mayer bologna
Poke Cake made with Jell-O
Libbyland Dinners

Reggie! Bar
Named after New York Yankees' right fielder Reggie Jackson and launched as a novely, Reggie! Bars were on sale for six years.

Hostess Chocodiles
Polynesian chicken salad
Salmon mousse
Cheese log appetizer
Gray Poupon Dijon Mustard

Tootsie Pop
So how many licks does it take to get to the center of a Tootsie Pop? 364, and that's official: it was tested on a "licking machine."

Cars of the 1970s

A decade of strikes, federal regulations, foreign imports, oil crises, safety and quality concerns: car sales were up overall, but the US industry was under pressure like never before. Iconic new models to debut include the Pontiac Firebird and the outrageous, gold-plated Stutz Blackhawk.

1940	**Chrysler New Yorker**
	When is a New Yorker not a New Yorker? The eighth generation of this upscale car bore little resemblance to the 1940 launch models. Yet in 1970, the New Yorker was barely middle-aged: they lived on until 1997.
1948	Ford F-Series
1959	General Motors Cadillac Coupe de Ville
1959	Chrysler Plymouth Valiant
1960	Chrysler Dodge Dart
1961	**General Motors Oldsmobile Cutlass**
	The Cutlass outsold any other model in US for four consecutive years, notching up nearly 2 million sales.
1962	General Motors Chevrolet Nova
1965	General Motors Chevrolet Caprice
1965	Ford LTD
1967	General Motors Pontiac Firebird
1968	BMW 2002
1970	Chrysler Dodge Challenger
1970	General Motors Chevrolet Monte Carlo
1970	General Motors Chevrolet Vega
1970	American Motors Corporation Hornet
1970	Ford Maverick
1971	Nissan Datsun 240Z
1971	**Stutz Blackhawk**
	These luxury automobiles started at a cool $22,000 ($150,000 today); the first car sold went to Elvis. Among the many other celebrity Blackhawk owners was Dean Martin; one of his three models sported the vanity plate DRUNKY. He crashed it.
1971	Ford Pinto
1973	Honda Civic
1975	Ford Granada
1978	Ford Fiesta

US Banknotes

The cast of US banknotes hasn't changed in your lifetime, giving you plenty of time to get to know them. (Although if you have a lot of pictures of James Madison and Salmon P. Chase around the house, you might want to think about a visit to the bank.)

Fifty cent paper coin (1862-1876) 🏧 Abraham Lincoln
These bills were known as "shinplasters" because the quality of the paper was so poor that they could be used to bandage leg wounds during the Civil War.

One dollar bill (1862-1869) 🏧 Salmon P. Chase
The US Secretary of Treasury during Civil War, Salmon P. Chase is credited with putting the phrase "In God we trust" on US currency beginning in 1864.

One dollar bill (1869-present) 🏧 George Washington
Some bills have a star at the end of the serial number. This means they are replacement bills for those printed with errors.

One silver dollar certificate (1886-96) 🏧 Martha Washington
Two dollar bill (1862-present) 🏧 Thomas Jefferson
Two dollar bills have a reputation of being rare, but there are actually 600 million in circulation in the US.

Five dollar bill (1914-present) 🏧 Abraham Lincoln
Ten dollar bill (1914-1929) 🏧 Andrew Jackson
Ten dollar bill (1929-present) 🏧 Alexander Hamilton
Twenty dollar bill (1865-1869) 🏧 Pocahontas
Twenty dollar bill (1914-1929) 🏧 Grover Cleveland
Twenty dollar bill (1929-present) 🏧 Andrew Jackson
Fifty dollar bill (1914-present) 🏧 Ulysses S. Grant
One hundred dollar bill (1914-1929) 🏧 Benjamin Franklin
The one hundred dollar bill has an expected circulation life of 22.9 years while the one dollar bill has an expected circulation life of just 6.6 years.

Five hundred dollar bill (1918-1928) 🏧 John Marshall
Five hundred dollar bill (1945-1969) 🏧 William McKinley
One thousand dollar bill (1918-1928) 🏧 Alexander Hamilton
One thousand dollar bill (1928-1934) 🏧 Grover Cleveland
Five thousand dollar bill (1918-1934) 🏧 James Madison
Ten thousand dollar bill (1928-1934) 🏧 Salmon P. Chase

Male Olympic Gold Medalists in Your Lifetime

These are the male athletes that have scooped the greatest number of individual and team gold medals at the Summer Olympics in your lifetime.

Michael Phelps (23) 🏅 Swimming (right)

Carl Lewis (9) 🏅 Athletics

Mark Spitz (9) 🏅 Swimming

For 36 years, Spitz's 7-gold-medal haul at the 1972 Munich Olympics was unbeaten; Michael Phelps finally broke the spell with his eighth gold in Beijing.

Matt Biondi (8) 🏅 Swimming

Caeleb Dressel (7) 🏅 Swimming

Ryan Lochte (6) 🏅 Swimming

Don Schollander (5) 🏅 Swimming

Gary Hall Jr. (5) 🏅 Swimming

Aaron Peirsol (5) 🏅 Swimming

Nathan Adrian (5) 🏅 Swimming

Tom Jager (5) 🏅 Swimming

Al Oerter Jr. (4) 🏅 Athletics

Four out of four: Oerter won Olympic gold medals in the discus in every Games from 1956–1968. He fought injuries that required him to wear a neck brace for the 1964 Tokyo Olympics—but he still set an Olympic record.

Greg Louganis (4) 🏅 Diving

Jason Lezak (4) 🏅 Swimming

John Naber (4) 🏅 Swimming

Jon Olsen (4) 🏅 Swimming

Lenny Krayzelburg (4) 🏅 Swimming

Matt Grevers (4) 🏅 Swimming

Michael Johnson (4) 🏅 Athletics

Once the fastest man in the world over 200 meters, Johnson took 15 minutes to walk the same distance in 2018 following a mini-stroke—but took it as a sign that he'd make a full recovery.

Harrison Dillard (4) 🏅 Athletics

Dillard—known as "Bones" for his skinny build—aspired to match the feats of his idol, Jesse Owens. And he did, becoming the only man to win gold as a sprinter and a hurdler.

Between 2000 and 2016, Michael Phelps won 28 Olympic medals, including 23 gold and 16 for individual events. That's 10 more than his nearest competitor, Larisa Latynina, a gymnast of the Soviet Union who took her last gold medal fifty years earlier.

Winter Olympics Venues Since You Were Born

Unless you're an athlete or winter sports fan, the Winter Olympics can slip past almost unnoticed. These are the venues; can you remember the host countries and years?

Lillehammer
Cortina d'Ampezzo
Oslo
Salt Lake City
Sapporo
Albertville
The last Games to be held in the same year as the Summer Olympics, with the next Winter Olympics held two years later.

Turin
Grenoble
Beijing
Sarajevo
Lake Placid
Sochi
Innsbruck (twice)
This usually snowy city experienced its mildest winter in 60 years; the army transported snow and ice from the mountains. Nevertheless, twelve years later, the Winter Olympics were back.

Squaw Valley
Nagano
St Moritz
The first Winter Olympics to be held for 12 years and named the 'Games of Renewal'; Japan and Germany were not invited.

Calgary
Vancouver
PyeongChang

Answers *Lillehammer: Norway, 1994; Cortina d'Ampezzo: Italy, 1956; Oslo: Norway, 1952; Salt Lake City: USA, 2002; Sapporo: Japan, 1972; Albertville: France, 1992; Turin: Italy, 2006; Grenoble: France, 1968; Beijing: China, 2022; Sarajevo: Yugoslavia, 1984; Lake Placid: USA, 1980; Sochi: Russia, 2014; Innsbruck: Austria, 1964; Squaw Valley: USA, 1960; Nagano: Japan, 1998; St Moritz: Switzerland, 1948; Calgary: Canada, 1988; Innsbruck: Austria, 1976; Vancouver: Canada, 2010; PyeongChang: South Korea, 2018*

Fashion in the Eighties

Eighties fashion was many things, but subtle wasn't one of them. Influences were everywhere from aerobics to Wall Street, from pop princesses to preppy polo shirts. The result was chaotic, but fun. How many eighties throwbacks still lurk in your closet?

Stirrup pants

Ralph Lauren

Ruffled shirts

Jean Paul Gaultier

Acid wash jeans

Stone washing had been around a while, but the acid wash trend came about by chance—Rifle jeans of Italy accidentally tumbled jeans, bleach, and pumice stone with a little water. The result? A fashion craze was born.

Camp collar shirt with horizontal stripes

Thierry Mugler

Oversized denim jackets

Scrunchies

"Members Only" jackets

Members Only military-inspired jackets were marketed with the tagline "When you put it on...something happens."

Paper bag waist pants

Pleated stonewash baggy jeans

Cut-off sweatshirts/hoodies

Vivienne Westwood

Azzedine Alaia

Shoulder pads

Dookie chains

Leg warmers

Bally shoes

Jordache jeans

Calvin Klein

Windbreaker jackets

Ray-Ban Wayfarer sunglasses

Popularized by Tom Cruise in the movie Risky Business.

Parachute pants

Jumpsuits

World Buildings

Some of the most striking and significant buildings in the world sprang up when you were between 25 and 50 years old. How many do you know?

1970	Cathedral of Brasília
1971	Näsinneula tower, Tampere, Finland
1972	Olympiastadion, Munich
1973	**The Sydney Opera House** The iconic Sydney Opera House sits on the tip of Bennelong Point—on a site that previously homed a tram shed.
1974	Shinjuku Mitsui Building, Tokyo
1975	First Canadian Place, Toronto
1976	The CN Tower, Toronto
1977	**The Centre Pompidou, Paris** The Centre Pompidou, known locally as Beaubourg, is considered the "inside-out" landmark—its structure and mechanical services are outside the building.
1978	Sunshine 60, Tokyo
1979	Kuwait Towers, Kuwait City
1980	Hopewell Centre, Hong Kong
1981	Sydney Tower
1982	First Canadian Centre, Calgary
1983	Teresa Carreño Cultural Complex, Caracas
1984	Deutsche Bank Twin Towers, Frankfurt
1985	Exchange Square, Hong Kong
1986	**Baha'i Lotus Temple, New Delhi** The Lotus Temple is open to all faiths to come worship, but no images, pictures, sermons, or even musical instruments are permitted.
1987	Fuji Xerox Towers, Singapore
1988	Canterra Tower, Calgary
1989	The Louvre Pyramid, Paris
1990	Bank of China Tower, Hong Kong
1991	One Canada Square, London
1992	Central Plaza, Hong Kong
1993	Westendstrasse 1, Frankfurt

Across the Nation

50

How many of these big national stories do you remember unfolding live on TV and radio?

- ✦ Waco siege of Branch Davidian compound ends in tragedy
- ✦ Bill Clinton becomes President
- ✦ Brady bill signed, requiring gun background checks
- ✦ World Trade Center bombed by terrorists
- ✦ Severe blizzard strikes most of country
- ✦ Beanie Babies launch
- ✦ Over $7 million stolen in Brinks armored car robbery
- ✦ Dallas Cowboys win the Super Bowl
- ✦ Tennis's Arthur Ashe dies of AIDS
- ✦ GM sues NBC News over rigging trucks to catch fire in story
- ✦ Intel ships Pentium chips
- ✦ Great Flood of Mississippi and Missouri Rivers
- ✦ Outbreak of hantavirus in the Southwest with several deaths
- ✦ Man opens fire on other commuters in passenger train, killing 6
- ✦ Ruth Bader Ginsburg confirmed to Supreme Court
- ✦ Wendy's Dave Thomas returns to high school to earn his GED
- ✦ DNA evidence exonerates innocent man on death row
- ✦ Women can wear pants in the US Senate chambers
- ✦ "The truth is out there" quote enters the language
- ✦ Human embryo cloned
- ✦ Sears closes its catalog department after 97 years
- ✦ Singer Prince changes his name to a symbol
- ✦ Baseball's Reggie Jackson retires
- ✦ Toronto Blue Jays win their 2nd consecutive World Series

Born this year:
- ♊ Singer Ariana Grande
- ♊ Singer Meghan Trainor
- ♊ Golfer Jordan Spieth

Around the World When You Turned 50

Here is the last set of international headlines in the book, and they're not so long ago (comparatively speaking).

- ✦ Canada elects woman as prime minister
- ✦ Haitian ferry sinks, killing 1,000
- ✦ Hundreds die in Bombay after bombs explode
- ✦ Japan hit by tsunami caused by off-shore earthquake
- ✦ Thousands die after earthquake hits India
- ✦ Oil tanker spill causes disaster in Scotland
- ✦ Earthquake hits Indonesia
- ✦ Apartment collapses in Malaysia
- ✦ IRA explodes bomb in London
- ✦ Buckingham Palace opens to public
- ✦ Nuclear accident occurs in Russia
- ✦ Rabin and Arafat sign peace agreement
- ✦ Tennis star Monica Seles stabbed
- ✦ Brush fire destroys Australian national park
- ✦ Massive riots kill 900 in Bombay
- ✦ Sri Lankan president is assassinated
- ✦ Eretria and Monaco join UN
- ✦ Hurricane Calvin hits Mexico
- ✦ Singapore elects president
- ✦ Hurricane Gert crosses Central America
- ✦ Cambodia restores monarchy
- ✦ China performs nuclear tests
- ✦ Burundi Civil War begins
- ✦ Nigerian government overthrown by coup
- ✦ Canadian prime minster resigns
- ✦ Israel and Vatican open relations
- ✦ Flooding kills thousand in South Asia
- ✦ Islamist militants set fire to hotel in Turkey

Kentucky Derby Winners

These are the equine and human heroes from the "most exciting two minutes of sport" during your thirties and forties. Did any of them make you rich?

1973 | **Secretariat (Ron Turcotte)**
Secretariat and Sham, both racing in the 1973 Kentucky Derby, had what still stand as the two fastest times ever in the race. Secretariat broke the track records at all three Triple Crown races (Kentucky Derby, Preakness Stakes, Belmont Stakes).

1974 | Cannonade (Angel Cordero Jr.)
1975 | Foolish Pleasure (Jacinto Vasquez)
1976 | Bold Forbes (Angel Cordero Jr.)
1977 | Seattle Slew (Jean Cruguet)
1978 | **Affirmed (Steve Cauthen)**
Affirmed won the Triple Crown, with Alydar finishing second in all three Triple Crown races.

1979 | Spectacular Bid (Ronnie Franklin)
1980 | **Genuine Risk (Jacinto Vasquez)**
Genuine Risk became the first female horse to win the Kentucky Derby since 1915.

1981 | Pleasant Colony (Jorge Velasquez)
1982 | Gato Del Sol (Eddie Delahoussaye)
1983 | Sunny's Halo (Eddie Delahoussaye)
1984 | Swale (Laffit Pincay Jr.)
1985 | Spend A Buck (Angel Cordero Jr.)
1986 | Ferdinand (Bill Shoemaker)
1987 | Alysheba (Chris McCarron)
1988 | Winning Colors (Gary Stevens)
1989 | Sunday Silence (Pat Valenzuela)
1990 | Unbridled (Craig Perret)
1991 | Strike the Gold (Chris Antley)
1992 | Lil E. Tee (Pat Day)
1993 | Sea Hero (Jerry Bailey)

World Series Champions Since You Were Born

These are the winners of the Commissioner's Trophy and the number of times they've been victorious in your lifetime.

- Detroit Tigers (3)
- New York Yankees (17)
- Cincinnati Reds (3)
- St. Louis Cardinals (7)
- Cleveland Indians (1)
- New York Giants (1)
- Brooklyn Dodgers (1)
- Milwaukee Braves (1)
- **Los Angeles Dodgers (6)**
  1988: Dodgers' Kirk Gibson, battling injuries, hit a game-winning home run in his only at-bat of the 1988 World Series.
- Pittsburgh Pirates (3)
- Baltimore Orioles (3)
- **New York Mets (2)**
  1969: The Mets had never finished above 9th in their division.
- Oakland Athletics (4)
- Philadelphia Phillies (2)
- Kansas City Royals (2)
- **Minnesota Twins (2)**
  1991: Both teams had finished in last place the previous season.
- Toronto Blue Jays (2)
- Atlanta Braves (2)
- Florida Marlins (2)
- Arizona Diamondbacks (1)
- Anaheim Angels (1)
- Boston Red Sox (4)
- Chicago White Sox (1)
- San Francisco Giants (3)
- **Chicago Cubs (1)**
  2016: The Cubs' first World Series win since 1908.
- Houston Astros (2)
- Washington Nationals (1)

Books of the Decade

By our forties, most of us have decided what we like to read. But occasionally a book can break the spell, revealing the delights of other genres. Did any of these newly published books do that for you?

1983	Pet Sematary by Stephen King
1983	Hollywood Wives by Jackie Collins
1984	You Can Heal Your Life by Louise Hay
1984	Money: A Suicide Note by Martin Amis
1985	The Handmaid's Tale by Margaret Atwood
1985	White Noise by Don DeLillo
1985	Lake Wobegon Days by Garrison Keillor
1986	It by Stephen King
1986	Wanderlust by Danielle Steele
1987	Patriot Games by Tom Clancy
1987	Beloved by Toni Morrison
1987	The Bonfire of the Vanities by Tom Wolfe
1988	The Cardinal of the Kremlin by Tom Clancy
1988	The Sands of Time by Sidney Sheldon
1989	Clear and Present Danger by Stephen R. Covey
1989	The Pillars of the Earth by Ken Follett
1990	The Plains of Passage by Jean M. Auel
1990	Possession by A.S. Byatt
1990	Four Past Midnight by Stephen King
1991	The Firm by John Grisham
1991	The Kitchen God's Wife by Amy Tan
1991	Scarlett by Alexandra Ripley
1992	The Bridges of Madison County by Robert James Waller
1992	The Secret History by Donna Tartt

Vice Presidents in Your Lifetime

The linchpin of a successful presidency, the best springboard to become POTUS, or both? Here are the men—and woman—who have shadowed the most powerful person in the world in your lifetime.

1941–45	Henry A. Wallace
1945	Harry S. Truman
1949–53	**Alben W. Barkley** He died of a heart attack during a speech at a political convention three years after the end of his term.
1953–61	Richard Nixon
1961–63	Lyndon B. Johnson
1965–69	Hubert Humphrey
1969–73	**Spiro Agnew (right)**
1973–74	Gerald Ford
1974–77	Nelson Rockefeller
1977–81	Walter Mondale
1981–89	**George H. W. Bush** He is only the second vice president to win the presidency while holding the office of vice president.
1989–93	**Dan Quayle** Quayle famously misspelled potato ("potatoe")
1993–2001	**Al Gore** This VP won the Nobel Peace Prize in 2007, following in the footsteps of two other former vice presidents.
2001–09	Dick Cheney
2009–17	Joe Biden
2017–20	**Mike Pence** In the 90s, Pence took a break from politics to become a conservative radio talk show and television host.
2020–	Kamala Harris

Spiro Agnew resigned in 1973, the second VP to quit in America's history (the first was John Calhoun in 1932). He stepped down after being charged with tax evasion and taking bribes. He covered his legal debts with a loan from friend Frank Sinatra. In 1983 he was compelled to repay $268,000: the money he had taken in bribes, plus interest.

British Prime Ministers in Your Lifetime

These are the occupants of 10 Downing Street, London, during your lifetime (not including Larry the resident cat). The list features three women (albeit one only lasting 45 days); three knights; and two who returned for a second go.

1940–45	Winston Churchill
1945–51	Clement Attlee
1951–55	**Sir Winston Churchill** Churchill was made an honorary citizen of the United States in 1963, one of only eight to receive this honor.
1955–57	Sir Anthony Eden
1957–63	**Harold Macmillan** Macmillan resigned following a scandal in which a minister was found to have lied about his relationship with a 19-year-old model.
1963–64	Sir Alec Douglas-Home
1964–70	Harold Wilson
1970–74	Edward Heath
1974–76	Harold Wilson
1976–79	James Callaghan
1979–90	**Margaret Thatcher** In 1994, Thatcher was working late in a Brighton hotel, preparing a conference speech. A bomb—planted weeks earlier by the IRA five stories above—detonated, devastating the hotel. Five were killed; Thatcher was unscathed. The conference went ahead.
1990–97	John Major
1997–2007	Tony Blair
2007–10	Gordon Brown
2010–16	David Cameron
2016–19	**Theresa May** Asked about the naughtiest thing she'd ever done, May said that she'd once run through a field of wheat.
2019–22	Boris Johnson
2022	Liz Truss
2022–	Rishi Sunak

Things People Do Now (Part 2)

Imagine your ten-year-old self being given this list of today's mundane tasks and habits—and the puzzled look on your face!

+ Listen to a podcast
+ Go "viral" or become social media famous
+ Watch YouTube
+ Track the exact location of family members via your smartphone
+ Watch college football playoffs
+ Have drive-thru fast food delivered to your door
+ Check reviews before trying a new restaurant or product
+ Use LED light bulbs to save on your electric bill
+ Wear leggings as pants for any occasion
+ Use hashtags (#) to express an idea or show support
+ Join a CrossFit gym
+ Use a Forever stamp to send a letter
+ Carry a reusable water bottle
+ Work for a company with an "unlimited" paid time off policy
+ "Binge" a TV show
+ Marry a person of the same sex
+ Take your shoes off when going through airport security
+ Take a selfie
+ Use tooth-whitening strips
+ Feed babies and kids from food pouches
+ Buy recreational marijuana from a dispensary (in some states)
+ Store documents "in the cloud" and work on them from any device
+ Clean up after your pets using compostable waste bags
+ Buy free-range eggs and meat at the grocery store

A Lifetime of Technology

It's easy to lose sight of the breadth and volume of life-enhancing technology that became commonplace during the 20th Century. Here are some of the most notable advances to be made in the years you've been an adult.

Year	Technology
1964	Plasma display
1965	Hypertext (http)
1966	Computer RAM
1967	Hand-held calculator
1969	Laser printer
1971	Email
1972	Video games console (Magnavox Odyssey)
1973	Mobile phone
1974	Universal Product Code
1979	Compact disc
1982	**Emoticons** The inventor of the smiley emoticon hands out "Smiley" cookies every September 19th—the anniversary of the first time it was used.
1983	Internet
1986	Mir Space Station
1988	**Internet virus** The first Internet worm was specifically designed to crack passwords. Its inventor was the son of the man who invented computer passwords.
1989	World Wide Web
1992	Digital hand-sized mobile phone
1995	**Mouse with scroll wheel** Mouse scroll wheels were developed primarily as a zoom function for large Excel sheets, but became more useable as a means of scrolling.
1998	Google
1999	Wi-Fi
2000	Camera phone
2001	Wikipedia
2004	Facebook
2007	Apple iPhone
2009	Bitcoin

The Biggest Hits When You Were 50

Fifty: an age when your musical taste is largely settled and modern music can lose its appeal…but how many do you know and how many do you like?

Haddaway 🎵 What Is Love
Lenny Kravitz 🎵 Are You Gonna Go My Way
Janet Jackson 🎵 That's the Way Love Goes
Mary Chapin Carpenter 🎵 Passionate Kisses
Snow 🎵 Informer
Spin Doctors 🎵 Two Princes
Alan Jackson 🎵 Chattahoochee
R.E.M. 🎵 Man on the Moon
Tag Team 🎵 Whoomp! (There It Is)
The Proclaimers 🎵 I'm Gonna Be (500 Miles)
Whitney Houston 🎵 I'm Every Woman
Vince Gill 🎵 I Still Believe in You
Rod Stewart 🎵 Have I Told You Lately
Peabo Bryson
and Regina Belle 🎵 A Whole New World
Lorrie Morgan 🎵 What Part of No
Aerosmith 🎵 Cryin'
UB40 🎵 (I Can't Help)
Falling in Love with You
4 Non Blondes 🎵 What's Up?
Toby Keith 🎵 Should've Been a Cowboy
Mariah Carey 🎵 Dreamlover
Meat Loaf 🎵 I'd Do Anything for Love
(But I Won't Do That)
Blind Melon 🎵 No Rain
Radiohead 🎵 Creep
Duran Duran 🎵 Ordinary World

Grand Constructions

Governments around the world spent much of the 20th century nation building (and rebuilding), with huge civil engineering projects employing new construction techniques. Here are some of the biggest built between the ages of 25 and 50.

1968	Nanjing Yangtze River Bridge, China
1970	Flathead Tunnel, US
1971	Azadi Tower, Iran
1972	Snowy Mountains Scheme, Australia
1973	Chesapeake Bay Bridge, US
1974	Charles de Gaulle Airport, France
1975	Orange-Fish River Tunnel, South Africa
1976	**Sonnenberg Tunnel, Switzerland** A 5,000-ft road tunnel built to double up as a 20,000-capacity nuclear shelter. Blast doors weigh 350 tons... but take 24 hours to close.
1977	Guoliang Tunnel, China
1978	West Gate Bridge, Australia
1979	Genting Sempah Tunnel, Malaysia
1980	Reichsbrücke, Austria
1981	Tjörn Bridge, Scandanavia
1982	Abu Dhabi International Airport, Abu Dhabi
1983	Queen Alia International Airport, Jordan
1984	Tennessee-Tombigbee Waterway, US
1985	Penang Bridge, Malaysia
1986	National Waterway 1, India
1987	Pikeville Cut-Through, US
1988	Great Seto Bridge, Japan
1989	Skybridge (TransLink), Canada
1990	Ningbo Lishe International Airport, China
1991	Fannefjord Tunnel, Norway
1992	Vidyasagar Setu Bridge, India
1993	Rainbow Bridge, Japan

Popular Food in the 1980s

The showy eighties brought us food to dazzle and delight.
Food to make us feel good, food to share and food to go.
Some innovations fell by the wayside, but many more can
still be found in our baskets forty years later.

Hot Pockets
Hot Pockets were the brainchild of two brothers, originally
from Iran. Their invention was launched as the Tastywich before
being tweaked to become the Hot Pockets enjoyed by millions.

Bagel Bites
Crystal Light
Steak-Umms
Sizzlean Bacon
Potato skins appetizers
Tofutti ice cream

Hi-C Ecto Cooler
Hi-C has been around for a very long time, but the Ecto Cooler
dates back to the Ghostbusters movie hype of the 1980s.

Hot buttered O's
Knorr Spinach Dip
Original New York Seltzer
Blondies

Blackened Redfish
The trend for blackening redfish prompted fish stocks
to drop so low that commercial fishing for the species
was banned in Louisiana.

Bartles & Jaymes Wine Coolers
Fruit Wrinkles
Stuffed mushrooms appetizers

TCBY Frozen Yogurt
TCBY originally stood for "This Can't Be Yogurt."

Sushi
Fajitas
Capri Sun
Jell-O Pudding Pops

Lean Cuisine frozen meals
Lean Cuisine is an FDA-regulated term, so all
Lean Cuisine frozen meals need to be within
the limit for saturated fat and cholesterol.

Eighties Symbols of Success

In the flamboyant era of Dallas and Dynasty there were many ways to show that you, too, had really made it. Forty years on, it's fascinating to see how some of these throwbacks are outdated or available to nearly everyone, while others are still reserved for today's wealthy peacocks.

BMW car

Cellular car phone

Rolex watch

Cosmetic surgery

In 1981 there were 1,000 liposuction procedures performed. That number increased to 250,000 by 1989.

VCR

"Home theater" projection TV

In-ground pool

AKC-registered dog

McMansion

Pagers/"beeper"

Aprica stroller

Home intercom system

Heart-shaped Jacuzzi tub

NordicTrack

This machine was originally called the Nordic Jock but was renamed due to compaints from women's rights groups.

Cruise vacation

Restaurant-standard kitchen appliances

A popular commercial stove produced enough heat to warm an average three-bedroom home. It was the energy equivalent of six residential stoves.

Ronald Reagan-style crystal jelly bean jar on your desk

Apple or Commodore 64 home computer

Volvo Station Wagon

Gordon Gekko-style "power suit"

Owning a horse or riding lessons for your children

Private jet

Tennis bracelet

Monogrammed clothes and accessories

Launched in 1980, the Apple III personal computer seen here went on sale for a hefty $4,000 and up, the equivalent of over $13,000 today. It didn't sell well and was soon withdrawn (unlike the Apple II, which went on to sell more than 5 million units).

The Transportation Coils

This novel issue of more than 50 definitive stamps first appeared on post in the early eighties, and became a favorite of collectors for its mono color engraved images of transportation methods past and present. Stamps carrying the printing plate number are particularly treasured. Here's a selection you may remember.

1 c 🖼 Omnibus

2 c 🖼 Locomotive

3 c 🖼 Handcar

4 c 🖼 **Stagecoach**

Coaches have been ferrying people and mail between US towns and cities since the late 18th century.

5 c 🖼 Motorcycle

5.5c 🖼 **Star Route Truck**

Star routes were 19th century mail routes on which carriers bid to make deliveries.

6 c 🖼 Tricycle

7.4 c 🖼 Baby Buggy

10 c 🖼 Canal Boat

11 c 🖼 Caboose

12.5 c 🖼 Pushcart

13 c 🖼 Patrol Wagon

15 c 🖼 Tugboat

17 c 🖼 Electric Auto

17 c 🖼 Dog Sled

17.5 c 🖼 Racing car

18 c 🖼 Surrey

20 c 🖼 Cog Railway

21 c 🖼 Railway Mail Car

23 c 🖼 Lunch Wagon

24.1 c 🖼 Tandem Bike

25 c 🖼 Bread Wagon

32 c 🖼 Ferry Boat

$1 🖼 **Sea Plane**

The US Navy bought its first sea plane in 1911: a Curtiss Model E, with a range of 150 miles.

Eighties Game Shows

By the eighties, game shows had their work cut out to compete against the popularity of new drama and talk shows. Still, an injection of celebrity glamour and dollar bills—alongside hours to be filled on new cable TV channels—ensured their survival. Here are the biggies.

Double Dare 🏆 (1986-2019)
Remote Control 🏆 (1987-90)
Scrabble 🏆 (1984-93)
The Price Is Right 🏆 (1972-present)
"Come on down!"—perhaps the best-known game show catchphrase of all time. One 2008 contestant was even happier than usual to do just that after 3 chips dropped into the Plinko all hit the $10,000 jackpot. Fluke? No, wires used to rig the result when filming ads hadn't been removed. She was allowed to keep the $30,000.

Family Feud 🏆 (1976-present)
Press Your Luck 🏆 (1983-86)
A show perhaps best remembered for the contestant Michael Larson, who memorized the game board and engineered a winning streak worth over $110,000. It wasn't cheating—Larson kept the winnings—but the game was swiftly reformulated.

Chain Reaction 🏆 1980-present)
Blockbusters 🏆 (1980-87)
Win, Lose, or Draw 🏆 (1987-90)
On The Spot 🏆 (1984-88)
Jeopardy! 🏆 (1964-present)
Card Sharks 🏆 (1978-present)
Wheel of Fortune 🏆 (1975-present)
Hostess Vanna White is estimated to clap 600 times a show; that's around 4,000,000 times since she began in 1982.

Fandango 🏆 (1983-88)
Body Language 🏆 (1984-86)
Jackpot! 🏆 (1974-90)

Popular Boys' Names

Not many of these boys' names were popular when you were born. But how many more of them are now in your twenty-first century family?

Jacob

Michael

Joshua

Joshua is very much a turn-of-the-century kind of name. He entered the Top 100 in 1972 and climbed to spend 25 years inside the top 5; now, he rarely makes the top 50.

Matthew

Andrew

Joseph

Ethan

Daniel

Christopher

Anthony

William

Nicholas

Ryan

David

Tyler

Alexander

John

James

Dylan

Zachary

Brandon

Jonathan

Samuel

Benjamin

Christian

Nathan

Rising and falling stars:

Aiden, Jayden, Colin and Landon are in; Victor and Trevor are out.

Popular Girls' Names

60

It's a similar story for girls' names: only Elizabeth featured in the 30 most popular names for your year of birth. How long will it be before we turn full circle and Shirley, Patricia and Barbara make a comeback?

Emily
Emily has held the top slot for 12 years since 1900—more than most. Though nobody comes close to Mary (54 years). Others: Linda (6), Lisa (8), Jennifer (15), Jessica (9), Ashley (2), Emma (6), Isabella (2), Sophia (3) and Olivia (since 2019).

Emma
Madison
Hannah
Olivia
Abigail
Alexis
Ashley
Elizabeth
Samantha
Isabella
Sarah
Grace
Alyssa
Lauren
Kayla
Brianna
Jessica
Taylor
Sophia
Anna
Victoria
Natalie
Chloe

Rising and falling stars:
Say hello to Arianna, Avery and Sofia; wave goodbye to Shelby and Jacqueline.

Game Show Hosts of the Seventies and Eighties

Here is the new generation of hosts: bow-tied, wide-smiled men to steer family favorites through tumultuous times. Astonishingly, one or two are still holding the cards.

John Charles Daly ➹ What's My Line (1950–1967)
Garry Moore ➹ To Tell The Truth (1969–1976)
Chuck Woolery ➹ Love Connection (1983–1994)
Bob Barker ➹ The Price Is Right (1972–2007)
Pat Sajak ➹ Wheel of Fortune (1981–)
Sajak took the crown for the longest-reigning game-show host of all time in 1983, when his 35-year reign surpassed that of Bob Barker as host of The Price is Right.

Peter Tomarken ➹ Press Your Luck (1983–86)
Gene Rayburn ➹ The Match Game (1962–1981)
Alex Trebek ➹ Jeopardy! (1984–2020)
At the time of his death in 2020, Trebek had hosted more than 8,200 episodes of the show.

Dick Clark ➹ Pyramid (1973–1988)
Richard Dawson ➹ Family Feud (1976–1995)
Peter Marshall ➹ Hollywood Squares (1966–1981)
Howard Cosell ➹ Battle of the Network Stars (1976–1988)
Marc Summers ➹ Double Dare (1986–1993)
Tom Kennedy ➹ Name That Tune (1974–1981)
Bert Convy ➹ Tattletales (1974–78; 1982–84)
Ken Ober ➹ Remote Control (1987–1990)
Jim Lange ➹ The Dating Game (1965–1980)
Wink Martindale ➹ Tic-Tac-Dough (1978–1985)
Art Fleming ➹ Jeopardy! (1964–1975; 1978–79)
Host for the original version, Fleming declined to host the comeback in 1983. His friend Pat Sajak took the job.

Jack Narz ➹ Concentration (1973–78)
Dennis James ➹ The Price Is Right (1972–77)
Jim Perry ➹ $ale of the Century (1983–89)
John Davidson ➹ Hollywood Squares (1986–89)
Ray Combs ➹ Family Feud (1988–1994)
Mike Adamle ➹ American Gladiators (1989–1996)

TV News Anchors of the Seventies and Eighties

The explosion in cable channels that began with CNN in 1980 brought a host of fresh presenters to join the ranks of trusted personalities that bring us the news. How many of them do you remember?

Dan Rather ♟ (CBS)
"Kenneth, what's the frequency?" Those were the words of the man who attacked Rather in 1986. It took a decade before the message was decoded; his assailant wanted to block the beams he believed TV networks were using to target him.

Peter Jennings ♟ (ABC)
Tom Brokaw ♟ (NBC)
Ted Koppel ♟ (ABC)
Bill Beutel ♟ (ABC)
Jessica Savitch ♟ (NBC)
Connie Chung ♟ (NBC)
Diane Sawyer ♟ (CBS/ABC)
Sam Donaldson ♟ (ABC)
Barbara Walters ♟ (ABC)
Walters was a popular pioneer; the first woman to co-host and anchor news programs, reaching 74 million viewers with her interview of Monica Lewinsky.

Frank Reynolds ♟ (ABC)
Jane Pauley ♟ (NBC)
Roger Grimsby ♟ (ABC)
Roger Mudd ♟ (CBS/NBC)
Garrick Utley ♟ (NBC)
Bernard Shaw ♟ (CNN)
Frank McGee ♟ (NBC)
Ed Bradley ♟ (CBS)
Larry King ♟ (CNN)
Kathleen Sullivan ♟ (ABC/CBS/NBC)
Jim Lehrer ♟ (PBS)
Robert MacNeil ♟ (PBS)
In 1963, MacNeil had a brief exchange of words with a man leaving the Texas School Book Depository; to this day, it is uncertain whether this was Lee Harvey Oswald.

FIFA World Cup: Down to the Last Four in Your Life

Here are the teams that have made the last four of the world's most watched sporting event in your lifetime (last year in brackets). The US men's team has reached the semifinals once, back in 1930.

Argentina ⚽ (2022, winner)
France ⚽ (2022, runner-up)
Croatia ⚽ (2022, 3rd)

During a 2006 match against Australia, Croatian player Josip Šimunić was booked three times due to a referee blunder.

Morocco ⚽ (2022, 4th)
Belgium ⚽ (2018, 3rd)
England ⚽ (2018, 4th)

In the run-up to the 1966 World Cup, hosted and won by England, the trophy was held to ransom. An undercover detective with fake banknotes arrested the crook; a dog named Pickles found the trophy under a bush.

Brazil ⚽ (2014, 4th)
Germany ⚽ (2014, winner)
Netherlands ⚽ (2014, 3rd)
Spain ⚽ (2010, winner)
Uruguay ⚽ (2010, 4th)
Italy ⚽ (2006, winner)
Portugal ⚽ (2006, 4th)
Turkey ⚽ (2002, 3rd)
Korean Republic ⚽ (2002, 4th)
Sweden ⚽ (1994, 3rd)
Bulgaria ⚽ (1994, 4th)
Poland ⚽ (1982, 3rd)
Russia ⚽ (1966, 4th)
Czech Republic (as Czechoslovakia) ⚽ (1962, runner-up)
Chile ⚽ (1962, 3rd)

The first foul occurred 12 seconds into the 'Battle of Santiago' between Chile and Italy. Punches were thrown and police intervened several times.

Serbia (as Yugoslavia) ⚽ (1962, 4th)
Hungary ⚽ (1954, runner-up)
Austria ⚽ (1954, third)

Books of the Decade

Our final decade of books are the bookstore favorites from your fifties. How many did you read...and can you remember the plot, or the cover?

1993	The Celestine Prophecy by James Redfield
1993	Like Water for Chocolate by Laura Esquivel
1994	The Chamber by John Grisham
1994	Disclosure by Michael Crichton
1995	The Horse Whisperer by Nicholas Evans
1995	The Lost World by Michael Crichton
1995	The Rainmaker by John Grisham
1996	Angela's Ashes by Frank McCourt
1996	Bridget Jones's Diary by Helen Fielding
1996	Infinite Jest by David Foster Wallace
1997	American Pastoral by Philip Roth
1997	Tuesdays with Morrie by Mitch Albom
1998	The Poisonwood Bible by Barbara Kingsolver
1998	A Man in Full by Tom Wolfe
1999	The Testament by John Grisham
1999	Hannibal by Thomas Harris
1999	Girl with a Pearl Earring by Tracy Chevalier
2000	Angels & Demons by Dan Brown
2000	Interpreter of Maladies by Jhumpa Lahiri
2000	White Teeth by Zadie Smith
2001	Life of Pi by Yann Martel
2001	The Corrections by Jonathan Franzen
2002	Everything is Illuminated by Jonathan Safran Foer
2002	The Lovely Bones by Alice Sebold

April 17, 1970: Jim Lovell is brought aboard a helicopter—the last of the three astronauts from the Apollo 13 mission to be lifted from the floating

Apollo Astronauts

Whatever your personal memories of the events, the moon landings are now woven into our national story—but not all of the Apollo astronauts who made the journey are equally well known. Twelve landed; twelve remained in lunar orbit. Gus Grissom, Ed White, and Roger B Chaffee died in training.

Landed on the moon:

Alan Bean

Alan Shepard
Shepard was the oldest person to walk on the moon at age 47.

Buzz Aldrin
Charles Duke
David Scott
Edgar Mitchell
Eugene Cernan
Harrison Schmitt
James Irwin
John Young
Neil Armstrong
Pete Conrad

Remained in low orbit:

Al Worden

Bill Anders
Anders took the iconic "Earthrise" photo.

Dick Gordon
Frank Borman
Fred Haise
Jack Swigert
Jim Lovell
Ken Mattingly
Michael Collins

Ron Evans
Made the final spacewalk of the program to retrieve film cassettes.

Stuart Roosa
On the Apollo 14 mission he carried seeds from 5 species of trees. They were planted across the US and are known as "Moon Trees."

Tom Stafford

US Open Tennis

And now it's the women's turn. Here are the tournament's victors when you were between the ages of the current "winning window": 16 years (Tracy Austin in 1979), and a venerable 42 years (Molla Mallory in 1926: she won eight times).

1959	Maria Bueno
1960–61	Darlene Hard
1962	Margaret Court
1963–64	Maria Bueno
1965	Margaret Court
1966	Maria Bueno
1967	Billie Jean King
1968	Virginia Wade
1969–70	**Margaret Court** Court won both the amateur and open championships in 1969.
1971–72	Billie Jean King
1973	**Margaret Court** In 1973, the US Open became the first Grand Slam tournament to offer equal prize money to male and female winners.
1974	Billie Jean King
1975–78	**Chris Evert** During the 1975 US Open, Evert beat her long-time rival Martina Navratilova in the semi-final. That evening, Navratilova defected to the United States and subsequently won the US Open four times.
1979	**Tracy Austin** 16-year-old Tracy Austin is the youngest US Open champion ever.
1980	Chris Evert
1981	Tracy Austin
1982	Chris Evert
1983–84	Martina Navratilova
1985	Hana Mandikova

The Biggest Hits
When You Were 60

We're not reaching back very far for these hits—but unless you're very young at heart, that probably means you won't know very many of them!

50 Cent 🎵 In da Club
Matchbox Twenty 🎵 Unwell
Kid Rock featuring Sheryl Crow 🎵 Picture
Alan Jackson and Jimmy Buffett 🎵 It's Five O'Clock Somewhere
Johnny Cash 🎵 Hurt
The Black Eyed Peas 🎵 Where Is the Love?
Stained 🎵 So Far Away
Beyoncé 🎵 Crazy in Love
Audioslave 🎵 Like a Stone
The Dixie Chicks 🎵 Landslide
Ludacris featuring Shawnna 🎵 Stand Up
Christina Aguilera 🎵 Beautiful
Toby Keith feat. Willie Nelson 🎵 Beer for My Horses
Evanescence 🎵 Bring Me to Life
Uncle Kracker feat. Dobie Gray 🎵 Drift Away
Justin Timberlake 🎵 Rock Your Body
Martina McBride 🎵 This One's for the Girls
Train 🎵 Calling All Angels
Counting Crows 🎵 Big Yellow Taxi
Kelly Clarkson 🎵 Miss Independent
John Mayer 🎵 Your Body Is a Wonderland
Trapt 🎵 Headstrong
Limp Bizkit 🎵 Behind Blue Eyes
Jason Mraz 🎵 The Remedy (I Won't Worry)

Things People Did When You Were Growing Up (Part 2)

Finally, here are more of the things we did and errands we ran as kids that nobody needs, wants, or even understands how to do in the modern age!

+ Buy cigarettes for your parents at the corner store as a child
+ Use a pay phone (there was one on almost every corner)
+ Join a bowling league
+ Collect cigarette or baseball trading cards
+ Get frozen meals delivered to your door by the iconic refrigerated yellow Schwan's truck
+ Attend "Lawn Faiths"/ ice cream socials
+ Chat with strangers over CB radio
+ Look up a phone number in the Yellow or White Pages
+ Visit the Bookmobile for new library books
+ Have a radio repaired at an appliance/electronics shop
+ Ride your bike without a helmet
+ Go to American Bandstand parties
+ Take part in a panty raid prank
+ Attend a sock hop
+ Get milk delivered to your door
+ Hang out with friends at a pizzeria
+ Use a rotary phone at home
+ Use a typewriter
+ Save your term paper on a floppy disc
+ Listen to LPs and the newest 45s
+ Care for a pet rock
+ Use a card catalogue to find books at the library
+ Attend a Sadie Hawkins Dance where girls invited the boys
+ Go disco roller skating

Made in United States
North Haven, CT
30 March 2023

34749370R00069

Nobody's journey down memory lane is quite the same, but this pocket-sized postcard from the past will show you the way. You'll discover the big news stories from your milestone birthdays; the music you grew up with; the games, food and cars of your childhood; habits lost and gained and even the species you've outlived! Blow the dust off a lifetime of memories—and enjoy the trip.

ISBN 978-1-912883-57-8

9 781912 883578